Able M U S E

A REVIEW OF POETRY, PROSE & ART

NUMBER 30
Winter 2022/2023

www.ablemuse.com

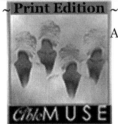

Able Muse

www.ablemuse.com

Editor	Alexander Pepple
Poetry Editor	Stephen Kampa
Associate Poetry Editors	Maryann Corbett, Nicole Caruso Garcia, Daniel Galef, Jean L. Kreiling
Nonfiction Editor	N.S. Thompson
Book Review Editor	Brooke Clark
Fiction Editor	Karen Kevorkian
Associate Fiction Editors	Lorna Brown, Tim Frank, Rob Wright
Editorial Board	Rachel Hadas, X. J. Kennedy, A. E. Stallings, Timothy Steele, Deborah Warren

Able Muse is published annually. Subscription rates—for individuals: $17.00 per year; libraries and institutions: $20 per year; single and previous issues: $21.95 + $4 S&H.

International subscription rates: $19.00 per year; single and previous issues: $21.95 + $6 S&H.
Subscribe online at www.ablemusepress.com or send a check payable to *Able Muse Review* to the snail mail address indicated below. (USD throughout. Online payment with Paypal/credit card.)

We read submissions in all genres from January 1 to July 15 yearly—previously unpublished manuscripts only. No simultaneous submissions. Online submissions ONLY. Submission guidelines available at: www.ablemuse.com/submit/.

Queries and other correspondence should be emailed to: editor@ablemuse.com
For paper correspondence, be sure to include a self-addressed, stamped envelope:

Attn: Alexander Pepple, Editor

Able Muse Review
467 Saratoga Avenue #602
San Jose, CA 95129

ISBN 978-1-77349-135-6 (paperback) / ISBN 978-1-77349-136-3 (digital)

ISSN 2168-0426

Cover image: *High on Water* by Anna Tarazevich

Cover & book design by Alexander Pepple

www.ablemuse.com
editor@ablemuse.com

Printed in the United States of America
Published in 2023 by Able Muse Press: www.ablemusepress.com

Alexander Pepple

Editorial

I N THIS ISSUE, featured poet Mary Jo Salter is capably interviewed by Stephen Kampa in a wide-ranging and revelatory exchange. Having served as the final judge of the 2012 Able Muse Book Award, Mary Jo is no stranger to *Able Muse*. And Stephen, who has appeared in many roles at *Able Muse*—contributor to the poetry section, assistant poetry editor, interviewer—is now our poetry editor, taking over from Richard Wakefield, who left for personal reasons, with our deep gratitude for his dedication and stellar work here.

Our featured art section explores the many aspects and implications of *Height*, as a theme, by worldwide artists.

Our regular sections include the usual fine poetry and poetry translation, from Amy Glynn, Gail White, Jenna Le, Jay Rogoff, Dan Campion, Natalie Staples, Tadeusz Dziewanowski, Daniel Bourne, and others. We have an abundant crop of stories of adventures of place or of the heart by Terese Coe, Silvia DiPierdomenico, R. S. Powers, and Thomas Mampalam—and we are proud to bring you Thomas's first-ever published story. And this is the first story with us from the eclectic Terese, who has been a regular contributor of poetry and poetry translation. Susan McLean reviews Alexandra Oliver's

Hail, the Invisible Watchman, while Brooke Clark and Peter Vertacnik each bring us a two-book review: Brooke reviews Alexis Sears's award-winning *Out of Order* and Luke Hathaway's *The Affirmations* poetry collections, while Peter takes on Daniel Brown's *Subjects in Poetry* guidebook and Boris Dralyuk's *My Hollywood and Other Poems* collection. Evan Fiscella brings us the hard-edged essay, "It's Just Weed," on addiction. Michael Hettich has the unique "Impressions and Collage" memoir/essay, while N. S. Thompson gives us his reading of John Keats's "On First Looking into Chapman's Homer."

We also present in this issue the winners of the eighth annual *Able Muse* contests.

For the 2022 Able Muse Write Prize for Fiction, as selected by final judge Dennis Must, congratulations to L. M. Brown. Then kudos to Brian Brodeur, winner of the 2022 Able Muse Write Prize for Poetry, selected by final judge Aaron Poochigian. This issue also includes the accomplished poetry of finalists Aaron Fischer and Donald Wheelock.

We also congratulate Amy Glynn for *Romance Language*, winner of the 2022 Able Muse Book Award as selected by final judge Rachel Hadas. Congratulations also to runner-up Gabriel Spera and finalists

Josh Dugat and David Livewell. They will all receive a standard Able Muse Press publication contract as well.

A special thank-you to the accomplished poets and writers who participated in our blind reading and shortlisting in the early judging stages. For the full list of winners, finalists, and other achievers, see page xvii.

I am pleased to announce that the 2023 run of *Able Muse* contests opens for submission at the very start of the new year. We are honored to announce at this time our three illustrious final judges: Chelsea Rathburn for the Write Prize for Poetry, Terese Svoboda for the Write Prize for Fiction, and David Yezzi for the Able Muse Book Award. Entry deadlines are provided in these pages, and details can be found at the *Able Muse* and Able Muse Press websites, ablemuse.com and ablemusepress.com.

We are also pleased to announce a brand new imprint of Able Muse Press called Many Words Press. Two new books are now in prerelease under this imprint: *Murder in Times Square (A Deirdre Mystery, Book One): A Novel* and *Advocatus Diaboli (The Catholic Themes, Book One): A Novel*, both novels by William Baer. Congratulations to Bill on his prolific and critically acclaimed output, and be sure to check out his new novels at the Able Muse Press or Many Words Press website, manywords.com, or wherever books are sold.

The submission period for our regular issues of *Able Muse*, print edition, opens at the very start of the new year and spans the yearly reading period of January 1 to July 15, per the guidelines available online at ablemuse.com/submit. If you'd like a chance to appear in these pages, send us your best work of poetry, fiction, nonfiction, book reviews, interviews, or art!

A special thank-you to our editors: fiction editor Karen Kevorkian, our new poetry editor Stephen Kampa, nonfiction editor N. S. Thompson, and book review editor Brooke Clark; our associate poetry editors Maryann Corbett, Daniel Galef, Nicole Caruso Garcia, and Jean L. Kreiling; and associate fiction editors L. M. Brown, Tim Frank, and Rob Wright. Immense thanks to our outgoing poetry editor, Richard Wakefield, for all his outstanding work and contributions to *Able Muse* and Able Muse Press!

We especially appreciate your continued support of *Able Muse*, *Eratosphere*, Able Muse Press, Word Galaxy Press, and Many Words Press—our brand new imprint. We hope you'll enjoy this issue as much as we've enjoyed bringing it to you.

The very best,

Alexander Pepple
—Editor

Strong Feather

~ Poems by Jennifer Reeser

978-1-77349-088-5 (paperback); 136 pp.

"What I love most about Jennifer Reeser's poems is their swagger. Can a feather be strong? You better believe it."—John Wilson, Englewood Review of Books + Marginalia Review of Books

"Jennifer Reeser's Strong Feather continues her personal legacy of applying classical technique to make another world visible. Like Countee Cullen of the Harlem renaissance, she is a master of rhyming forms that present life beyond the expected edges of formal verse."
—Arthur Mortensen, Expansive Poetry Online

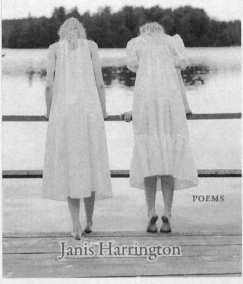

How to Cut a Woman in Half

~ Poems by Janis Harrington

78-1-77349-094-6 | Paperback; 96 pp.

". . . . so compelling that once I started reading, I couldn't stop."
—Cecilia Woloch, author of Tsigan: The Gypsy Poem *and* Earth

". . . beautifully contain painful restraint and the breaking of sorrow."
—April Ossmann, author of Anxious Music *and* Event Boundaries

"A beautiful and healing read."
—Rebecca Foust, author of Paradise Drive *and* Only

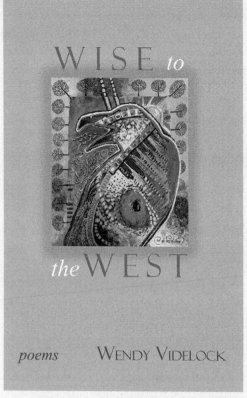

Wise to the West
~ Poems by **Wendy Videlock**
978-1-77349-113-4 (paperback); 116 pp.

[Videlock's] craft is worthy. Her delicate turning of a line is as breathtaking as it is brief.
— *Jeffrey P. Beck*, Borderlands

The wordplay is irresistible.
— *Ann Drysdale*, The Shit Creek Review

[A] playfulness with the language and an undeniable wit that [is] difficult not to enjoy.
— *Marissa Fox*, Gadfly Online

At play in the spacious fields of her wit and down-to-earthiness.
— *Matt Sutherland*, Foreword Reviews

Just as one can walk into a room in an art gallery, see a painting for the first time and immediately recognize it as a Van Gogh or a Cezanne, one immediately knows when one is reading Videlock.
— *Jeremy Telman*, Valparaiso Review

Oxblood
~ Poems by **Nicole Caruso Garcia**
978-1-77349-105-9 (paperback); 94 pp.

"... so fierce and yet so vulnerable that it demands to be read in one sitting ... Garcia's themes are intense, but their impact is made stunning by her mastery of craft."—Anna M. Evans, author of *Under Dark Waters: ... the Titanic* and *Sisters & Courtesans*

"This is a book of Ovidian elaboration and imagination ... In poetry of the highest quality, verse that never fails to be first rate, the savagery of sexual assault is stitched indelibly."—Mark Jarman, author of *The Heronry: Poems* and *Dailiness: Essays*

"Damn, this book comes at you, from the first sound to the last syllable ... *Oxblood*, beautiful with brokenness, is a fierce and fearless debut by a breathtakingly gifted and badass poet."—Matt W. Miller, author of *Tender the River* and *The Wounded for the Water*

ABLE MUSE BOOK PRIZE

2023 Able Muse Book Award
for poetry

» **$1000 prize** *for winning manuscript*

» **Publication** *by Able Muse Press*

» *All poetry styles welcome (metrical & free verse)*

» **Blind judging** *by the final judge*

» **Final Judge**: *David Yezzi*

» **Entry Deadline:** *March 31, 2023*

**GUIDELINES & ENTRY INFORMATION
AVAILABLE ONLINE AT:**

www.ablemusepress.com

CONTENTS

FEATURED POET

FEATURED ART

FICTION

2022 Write Prize for Fiction ▪ Winner

POETRY

2022 WRITE PRIZE FOR POETRY ▪ WINNER

2022 WRITE PRIZE FOR POETRY ▪ FINALISTS

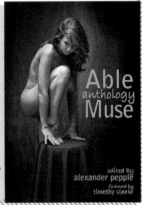

Congratulations to the 2022
Able MUSE
CONTEST WINNERS

2022 ABLE MUSE WRITE PRIZE	2022 ABLE MUSE BOOK AWARD

FICTION
Final Judge: **Dennis Must**

WINNER
- L. M. Brown
"Looking for Anna"

Honorable Mention
- Trish Lindsey Jaggers

FINALISTS
- Bruce Johnson, J. S. Kierland, Victoria Mack, Suzanne C Martinez, Mark Rhodes, Roger Sedarat, Alan Sincic, Rob Wright

POETRY
Final Judge: **Aaron Poochigian**

WINNER
- Brian Brodeur:
"On Mistaking a Stranger for a Dead Friend"

FINALISTS
- Aaron Fischer, Donald Wheelock

HONORABLE MENTIONS
- Daniel E. Haar (twice), B. Fulton Jennes, Brett Reid, David M. Sloan

POETRY MANUSCRIPT
Final Judge: **Rachel Hadas**

WINNER
- Amy Glynn
Romance Language

RUNNER-UP
- Gabriel Spera:
Twisted Pairs

FINALISTS
- Josh Dugat:
Great and Small (was *Skull Muscle*)
- David Livewell:
Pass and Stow (was *A Vase in Lockdown*)

HONORABLE MENTIONS
- Renee Emerson: *The Work of Breathing*
- Ceridwen Hall: *Acoustic Shadows*
- Kathryne Lim: *Dream of Being*
- Eric Meub: *Watch Repair*
- Hilary Sallick: *Raptor*
- Jennifer Judge Yonkoski: *Here's What I Mean*

BOOKS FROM THE RUNNER-UP AND FINALISTS ALSO COMING SOON FROM ABLE MUSE PRESS!

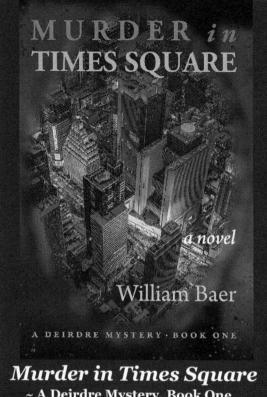
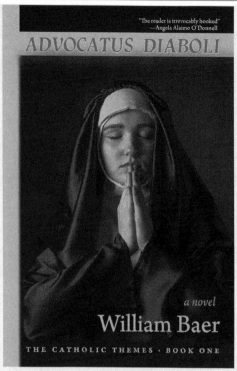

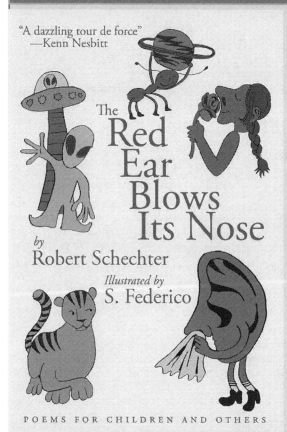

Jenna Le

The Implorer

This figurine of bronze
cast by Camille Claudel,
known as Auguste Rodin's
mentee and, for a spell,

his lover, is most striking
for being non-erotic—
desexed—despite depicting
a kneeling nude, lordotic

trunk outthrust at an angle
headlong, precipitous,
arms outstretched not to strangle
one who broke faith, but just

to make a strangled gesture,
a soundless, ground-out groan,
the hauntings that oppress her
knowable to her alone.

Jay Rogoff

Averted Vision

. . . peering with one eye through a telescope at the night sky: dim things disappear if you look right at them. Deep-space observers combat this effect by employing averted vision, meaning that they look slightly away from the objects of their attention. Averted vision is the deepest vision.
—Timothy Ferris

Averted vision is the deepest vision;
we're blinded where the retina strikes a nerve.
Believing all you see is superstition.

Since gazing at raw bodies risks derision,
sneak barest peeks, letting your eyebeams swerve.
Averted vision is the deepest vision,

the coyly carnal stare cooked up for Titian,
whose naked Venus throws you a naked curve,
believe you me. See? No superstition

restrains her fingers' manual transmission
whipping desire from virginal reserve.
She averts her vision, but her deepest vision

sees through foreplay to the firm collision
of flesh and no flesh. Students, observe.
Believing all you see is superstition

inserts you in the forefront of tradition,
where smiling nudes mature into *chefs d'œuvre*.
Averted vision is the deepest vision.
Believing all, you see, is superstition.

Amy Glynn

Space Is the Final Frontier

The pattern's partial,
Lord, its pointillism
incomplete: to plot
this form
requires more flame:
this is still
a constellation
without a name.

—Richard Kenney

At this point, nothing's truly off the table.
Venus is conjunct Mars in Aries—it's

a gambler's placement. Everything just . . . fits,
however transitory and unstable;

everything's ours and filthy with potential.
Like puzzle pieces, we'll say later, blown

away by how one moment writes its own
little master class on *force majeure*. Essential

story points emerge in filaments
of glitter: one or two that demarcate

the roofline, or the firmament, intense
enough to see in daylight; then, a great

proliferation littering the field
at dusk. Out of which certain truths emerge,

an archetypal, overwhelming surge
of myth and implication. What's revealed

is, more than anything, a timeless story
of how we conjure meaning from those chance

alignments, accidents of circumstance,
flashes of recognition of a glory

we need to feel has implicated us.
We say *inevitable*, point out the yod

our birth charts share, the thumbprint divots God
pressed on both our fontanelles at once.

Think of the first time, if you can pin down
what that even was—we were thirteen; we were

infants in San Anselmo; there's a blur
of images from other lifetimes: brown

eyes watching for the slice of light that cuts
the hardwood just before the bedroom door

opens; glass fracturing against the floor
of a room you know but don't; a parakeet's

small riot of green and yellow feathers (whose
pet bird was that? It talked.) Why must it mean

something that I have memories that are
not mine, or that we're haunted by the same

dream where a child with bronze curls says her name
must be spoken? Staggering out of a bar

in Cap Hill, we are dazzled by the cold
clarity of the air, eyes drawn upward by a spate

of brilliances, diamond-cut-diamond spit-
fire daughters of Atlas burning with an old

lament for things that never change, but should.
In eighty-nine years we will meet again,

this time in Jaipur. Me: twelve, over men
already. You: sixteen, shy, with good

teeth and lean thighs and no idea how
to start a conversation. But despite

ourselves we'll share a certain thrill when night
falls and Elektra rises. We will grow

attached. It will seem oddly foreordained.
Things will go sideways anyway. We'll say

it's written. We'll believe it, too. Today
Venus squares Pluto, indicating strained

relations stemming from intensity
of feeling. We do not yet understand

how deep this goes. How could we? One dim strand
emerges. Then, a radiant tapestry.

Silvia DiPierdomenico

The Ledger

To Grace and Betty, and to Rudi, Marie, and all the friends who have shown the way forward

IT WAS ONLY a month ago, after chemotherapy number five, that the prayer cards started to arrive in the mail. Some days they came three at a time, their appearance always the same: my Brooklyn address in my mother's familiar boxy handwriting, punctuated here and there with stickers of animals and flowers. It was unusual to receive a Hallmark or an American Greetings card from my mother. More typically the cards are from organizations that help the visually impaired or the mentally ill. St. Jude Charity and the Christian Appalachian Project are two charities to which she is particularly devoted.

Aside from charity, my mother believes in thrift. She saves for disaster. I grew up in a house in Massachusetts that boasted a twelve-by-fifteen-foot cement basement stockroom. A testament to her disaster preparedness, it is where she stacks foodstuffs from floor to ceiling. Shelved alongside six others of its kind, each canned good stares out like a face in a police lineup.

My mother is a former bank employee who likes making lists and recording transactions. As long as I can remember she's kept a ledger of household expenses. With a knack for numbers, she easily adds and subtracts large sums in her head. Her ledger is organized in the same way that the *Chemotherapy and You* booklet handed out by the hospital divides everything into sections. The only difference is that instead of registering details in an official-looking blotter, my mother writes down each daily expense in a yellow Mead spiral notebook. As in a mall directory, there are specific groupings:

Gas – Shell / $25
Dry Cleaning – Pam's Laundry / $15.75
Groceries – The Big Bunny, double
    coupons / $87.34
Cleaning Supplies – Spag's / $33.21

It isn't just things that get recorded, but people, too. My sisters and I each have a tally of expenditures. Like a bar tab with no end point, there are specific entries for each one of us: Clothing, Shoes, School Supplies, Education, Dental, Medical, Birthday Parties, Weddings.

Always on the lookout for a special deal, my mother buys particular groceries not because of any distinct food preference or craving, but out of her fealty to coupons. Any sales event, white sale, jumble sale, sale-a-thon, or sales marathon radiates a magical attraction for my mother similar to the hopeful high derived from believing in Santa Claus or the Tooth Fairy. On Saturdays, as a respite from the household chores, she snips coupons for nonperishables like Chef Boyardee, Kraft Macaroni and Cheese, or Spam. Like a library, the cement stockroom is organized by type: condiments, sauces, jams, tinned vegetables, fruit in heavy syrup, vinegars, and soft drinks. More than any other room in the house, that food pantry reveals my mother's commitment to categories.

It is the way she feels about her daughters. Growing up, I was the smart one. My older sister was the ambitious one, my middle sister the pretty one, and my younger sister the baby. When she turns her eyes on you, my mother has a way of looking directly without taking in who you really are. She shrinks individuals down to handling size by summing them up in quick catchall phrases like "tough old bird" or "amazon" or "supermodel." You can see that she only ever takes notice of people or things she can label and shelve like the bargain-priced canned goods she collects. She keeps emotions like love and humor tightly bundled in the same way that she systemizes the six-inch high towers of canceled checks on her desk.

Assured by her investment in the *Encyclopedia Britannica* and the *Mayo Clinic Family Health Book*, my mother doesn't see any need for internet access or for cable. Maybe because of this and the fact that we only talk over the phone once a month, she has a hard time remembering what kind of cancer I have. "I'm gonna write it down so I don't forget. How do you spell it?"

Now, on the day before chemotherapy number six, my mother calls with the news of two deaths. Her voice expands into the phone, "Two weeks ago I was very upset. It upset the hell out of me. The man I would have married if I hadn't married your father fell off the roof of the house he was working on. He fell nine feet. It makes you think. The guy I would have married died. When I found out, I said to myself: I would have been a widow today."

"You almost married someone else?"

"There's no need to talk about it. That's life. And it isn't *fair* either. I had more bad news yesterday. My cousin Nancy died this week. You know she beat the cancer once before when she was in her twenties, and in July, exactly a month before my wedding anniversary, it came back. By the time they figured out what was wrong, it was everywhere. I'd been calling her every day since I found out she was sick. She'd been living in Florida and her mother moved in with her to take care of her. After Thanksgiving the family brought her home to Canada. I'd been sending her funny cards each week. You know, just greeting cards with jokes. It made me feel good to hear from her mother that she appreciated those cards from me."

"Are you going to the funeral?"

"I wanted to go. But I cut my foot. I can't fly. I was going into the chapel early the other morning and the door closed on my heel. You know I'm always going at a dead run. There was blood everywhere when I took my tights off. I can hardly put a shoe on, never mind get on a plane." After a short pause my mother's voice came again over the phone, hurried, as if she were trying to catch her breath. "Well, I would have wanted to go. I would have done it for her father. I really loved him." I don't ask questions of my mother, so I don't ask why she wouldn't have done it for Nancy.

Later on, toward the evening, when I was flipping through one of the patient handbooks, something about the table of contents started me thinking about my mother and our phone calls. How she had a way of bringing up other things, changing the subject when you were talking to her or telling her something about yourself. Like an office clerk stuffing envelopes for a mass mailing, her mind had the habit of drifting over to events she'd heard about or seen on TV. This did not necessarily reflect how my mother felt about our relationship, and I

knew she was proud of my accomplishments. Sometimes, when discussing old Hollywood movies, we were in sync, but without warning the lightheartedness would fade and the prospect of friendship dissipated.

After all the phone calls during the six months of treatment, it was like we were still always meeting for the first time, two people who kept up a routine of politeness without getting to know each other better. But she tries. Like the prayer cards, her litany of platitudes is her way of reaching out. Time and again she recites the same three: "Look on the bright side," "He who knows more, does more," "Don't look a gift horse in the mouth." I felt sorry for the girl she must have been: the lonely only child of a sickly, widowed, immigrant mother.

As a teenager, I blurred the details of my life in order to avoid any confrontation with my mother. Craving autonomy, I concealed opinions I knew she would find objectionable. I hid from her outrage by retreating into books; the less we talked, the easier it was to escape her expectations. As a result, during college I returned home only on school breaks. The year after graduation, I moved to New York. Though I lived in a one-bedroom apartment with my boyfriend, I never revealed this fact to my mother. Seeing the fifth-floor walk-up in Manhattan didn't matter to her; there was no prospect of being caught out in the lie. I felt guilty for blunting the truth but I knew my mother would not come to visit. Instead, she sent care packages full of things she imagined I needed: boxes of pasta, aluminum foil, paper towels, and Ziploc bags. In January each year the packages included a birthday gift picked up at her local thrift shop. It struck me as odd that though these were presents—a waffle iron, elbow-length satin gloves, a glass owl ashtray, a frayed terry cloth bathrobe— they seemed chosen at random with no knowledge of my specific taste. I didn't look forward to these gifts. And when I sorted my belongings for the move from Manhattan to Brooklyn, I packed them up in a box for Salvation Army donation.

After being diagnosed with lymphoma, I thought I would continue studying for my doctorate in literature, but sticking with the chemotherapy protocol was harder than I had envisioned. Applying for research grants, going to the library each day, and writing seemed irrelevant. I wanted more than anything to get through treatment without losing any weight or having to be hospitalized. And so each week I prepared calorie-rich meals with polenta and sweet potatoes. To cleanse my liver of the chemotherapy drugs, I drank milk thistle tea and ate beets. I hid from other passengers on the subway the fact I was bald.

Being a cancer patient was my obligation now: the four-hour monthly infusions at the doctor's office, the follow-up blood tests, the CAT and PET scans. "Don't be hasty," my mother said, when I told her about quitting the PhD program. "Education-wise, you've already exceeded by forty thousand dollars your sisters, a few more years of studying will go by quickly."

My mother has a mythical way of counting time. On Sunday nights, when I was a child, at the beginning of each school year, the dinner dishes having been washed and put away, she would begin shortening the school week. "Well, tomorrow is already Monday, first day of school, so it will go by fast. Tuesday will be busy with after-school projects, so that means it is technically already Wednesday. And Wednesday is called hump day for a reason—you can see over Thursday into Friday—so the first week of school is already more than half over."

It has been eight months since I last saw my mother. She came in August, staying for an afternoon. In the course of falling ill, being hospitalized, getting diagnosed, and completing chemotherapy, two hundred forty-three days have gone by. Somehow, it was easier with distance between us to feel an affinity with her, a closeness created by childhood memories. I thought of her seated at her treadle sewing machine, surrounded by scraps of fabric and colorful thread, pumping the cast iron lever with her foot as she talked. Unlike other mothers I saw around school and at church, my mother never wore pants. She was the sort to take a half hour drive to a discount store to buy notions and fabric for making dresses. She mail-ordered McCall's and Butterick sewing patterns. I hadn't found her industriousness surprising; she rarely was idle. In addition to sewing her own clothing, she created an entire wardrobe for my beloved doll Emily— jumpsuits, sundresses, a raincoat, pajamas, and even a red swimsuit. I remembered the wonder I felt in watching her trace the pattern before cutting the fabric that she then ran under the needle of the antique Singer. Holding up the finished doll-size garment, my mother would smile, and I would laugh, marveling at the mystery of transformation.

I am thankful my mother can't see how I've changed: moon face, faded eyebrows, and the catheter—a solid lump in my chest. Alarmed by my hairlessness, I'm disappointed each time I catch my reflection in the mirror. I consider if in the time apart my mother's brown hair has begun to gray. My own hair fell out in patches after the first round of chemotherapy. The doctor assures me it will grow back on its own, but not too long ago, I received an envelope in the mail containing several coupons for popular hair regrowth shampoos. On a Post-it my mother had written, "Just in case!"

For my mother it is hard to have a twenty-nine-year-old daughter with cancer. It's one thing to save for a rainy day and store up provisions, but you can't save up for cancer. Unlike canned goods that come with a *best before* date stamped on the lid to guarantee the food will be edible when you finally get around to eating it, chemotherapy comes with no such guarantee.

But the cost is assured. The cost of my illness is readily quantifiable. It is no strain on my mother's knowledge. The sum of medical expenses satisfactorily fits in the yellow ledger under the heading "Cancer Treatment." This likely comes as a comfort to my mother who cannot uncover how the cancer cells gained access to the immediate family.

Even now, as I set about organizing my desk, I still don't know how it happened. There are no answers in the brightly colored hospital brochures I pull from the far corners of the desk. For the first time since the diagnosis, I've pictured my older self, performing routine activities: going to the movies, attending a dinner party, taking a walk in the sunshine with no need to cover my head. I looked forward to such unremarkable things as I sifted through relics accumulated over the last year: a set of French stationery, two Cross ballpoint pens, scenic postcards never sent from a trip to France, and a dozen prayer cards from my mother. These I turn over in my hands, noticing that aside from the stickers dotting the envelopes, the cards betray no sign of personalization beyond the usual signature, "Best Love, Ma." As I contemplate whether to throw them away, I trace the letters of my mother's closing. It is a declaration that is not compatible with the person my mother is on the phone, a declaration of intimacy that doesn't fit with my experience of her. And yet I gather up the prayer cards, compressing their mass with a rubber band. Then from the closet in the hall, I take a box and store them inside. I place the box in the middle drawer of my desk, locking the cards away as proof of our connection.

Mike Chasar

Stealing Auden's Slippers

Call number YCAL MSS 580

In my dream, I am sitting in front of Box 26
of the James Merrill Papers at the Beinecke Rare Book & Manuscript Library.
I am on fellowship, and I have additional and generous
support from my home institution.
Everyone thinks I am writing a book on the known and unknown,
and I am there on the premise of studying Merrill's use of the Ouija board.

Truth be told, I'm not entirely uninterested in JM's use of the Ouija board,
but I can't justify spending twenty-six
hours in connecting airports, not knowing what I know
of spirits and airplane hygiene, and then two weeks of the library's
fellowship funds to argue for the ideomotor effect as a modern epistemological
    institution.
Too many people have been too generous

for me to clutter my unconscious with something that's insufficiently *sui generis*.
In my dream, therefore, I lift the crisp-cornered cardboard
lid of the beige crate's tuition
and remove from underneath JM's cat's collar the pair of slippers: Box 26.
They are like nothing else in the library.
They are like nothing, in fact, that I've ever known

and nothing, I think, that I will ever know.
Perhaps he wore them with his baize blazer on the New York subway, generous
paisley interior comforting his corns on the way to the library!
Or to China—or to lunch with Chester! Or, bored

in the middle of winter late in life, he wore them at home remembering how, at 26,
he and Christopher lounged in nothing but open robes and frank intuition.

I am not, nor have I ever been, affiliated with an Ivy League institution.
My work on the known and unknown is by and large unknown.
I will never have a Box 1 let alone a Box 26.
However kind and patient and generous
I am with my family, friends, students, and lovers, no board
of well-heeled trustees will approve the acquisition of my cat's collar for the library,

nor do I need the planchette's prosthetic heart to talk with the dead, to library,
file, or tag the blood-red, paisley-lined institution
of my life. Reader, I have lived a dream, and in that dream, six feet of board
and the curt unknown
is more than a generous
return when you fall in love mid-life and once again are made to feel 26,

and so, in my dream, front desk librarians are always in love, bored
of institutions, even more bored of Box 26,
and thus they are knowing, then generously unknowing, then known.

Tadeusz Dziewanowski

Natural Selection

After the elimination of all worthless specimens
There arose at last a species able to feed on empty packages
Of potato chips, that gladly watched ads about hemorrhoid creams
And transmissions of the latest riots on Mars.
This species loved to take walks with its neighbor on a leash
And learned to reproduce by liking on Facebook.
It fell in love with both gorgeous pixels and the morning smog.
Luckily, God never got involved.

— *Translated from the Polish[1] of Tadeusz Dziewanowski*
by Daniel Bourne

---

1   See "Translation Notes" on page 121 for the original Polish poem.

Evan Fiscella

It's Just Weed

A LIGHT IN THE DARKNESS, of salvation, terror. A halo, the white of an angel. God's grace lasts for six seconds or so. The beacon disappears, smoke departing barely visible lips, dancing with the steam of a shower. A hit. The pattering of water shelters a cough, the muffled thump of a pen falling on a fluffy mat. I pull aside glass, head light, stepping into that basin, the warmth of water mingling with that of my chest. Everything, for one blissful moment of peace, is forgotten; existence is halted. It was the eighth hit of the night.

They say weed is not addictive.

I lie on a park bench, my first love in my arms. Distant stadium lights disrupt the night sky, a violent illumination that clings to my mind. It feels as if we are the act, the main attraction. She leans back, pulling a disposable out of her hoodie pocket. A light in the darkness, for a moment, then smoke blows from her lips. That image lives in my memory, the quick glance her round brown eyes made to see if we were alone, the secrecy with which she covered the pen

with her small hands. Discreet, hidden. A moment of silence, then I ask: *What does weed feel like?* It feels warm, she says. It's calming, soothes your anxiety. It is like a thin blanket that covers your perception, not the violent inhibition of alcohol. It's a presence in your head, cloudy, yet comforting. You laugh easily, escape the grasp of boredom. It's hard to think, but that doesn't matter; you're happy. She was a bit of a poet, I admit. *I might try it sometime.* She smiles.

We sit on some concrete steps off a side road. Night, of course. The clamor of traffic paints the background despite the hour. She holds a joint in one hand, a lighter in the other. I'm nervous. Hyperaware. She fumbles with the lighter. *Click. Click.* The wind is strong, fighting the flame. *Click.* She brings the joint to her lips, inhales. It's beautiful, that orange halo that draws the eyes. The way the hemp wrapping surrenders to the flame on inhale, the way it lazily smokes on release. I love it, the act, the smell. She blows smoke into the air, that familiar ballet in the sky. A pirouette, a jeté?

I find the joint in my hand. I laugh. *I don't know how to inhale.* A grin, white teeth stark against the darkness. She grasps my hand that holds the joint, bringing it to her lips. The halo intensifies, hemp flees. She brings her lips to mine and exhales. The acrid tang fills my mouth, forced into virgin lungs. It burns, yet feels light, feels whole. We kiss, for a moment. Her mouth, breath tastes of bud. I've never before had the taste, the smell, the sensation. I exhale, coughing. She laughs. *That's how you know it worked.* The joint trades hands a few more times. My head begins to feel heavy, cloudy, my chest warm. It's hard to think.

She says weed is not addictive. It's just to chill out. Maybe she could get something for anxiety, but that's hard. Expensive. You have to find a therapist, schedule a time and you know how busy she is and she doesn't have a car so she'll have to pay for an Uber and she really wanted to DoorDash some boba which is fifteen with tax. Oh, and to take some pills that make you gain weight, are a pain to swallow and remember, and you feel numb, alienated. You can't be happy like that. Weed is a plant, it's natural, it's meant to be smoked, it tastes good, why would she walk down that white hallway and stand before the psychiatrist who speaks in medical jargon and the psychiatrist who greets your tears with tissues instead of a hug and the psychiatrist whose cold eyes think of that three hundred dollar paycheck at the end of the hour. That smile of triumph when they solve the grand riddle of your panic disorder, that secret satisfaction that you fit into diagnostic criteria like a piece

in a puzzle. The way their eyes glaze over when you tell them of the girl in high school who kissed you with those glossed lips that tasted like strawberries and then called you fat and ugly and an illegal and how you cried that night and ravaged your throat from the shrieks. Your plug, really your uncle, for he's your mom's best friend and has been with you since you were five and gave you small packets of blueberry bubble gum on those warm Friday afternoons before he and your mom went into the small garage and smoke billowed out like fog—he's given you weed since you were thirteen and it worked then, it's worked every day. After all, it's just medicine.

I walk into a smoke shop, glancing at a "21 and older" decal. Adrenaline. Panic courses through me. I leave today, I need it now. The shop is decorated with disposables, rigs, carts, edibles. I walk up to the counter, stare at the cashier, into a smile that reaches cold eyes. *I'm looking for a cart and battery.* Rehearsed, poorly, obvious. He nods; do you have the app? Some stupid passcode, like they need an excuse to sell to minors. I think of a friend, one I always regarded as an addict, an outcast. What he told me. *Yes. It's called clover.* He grins at me, eyes alight. Genuine. I walk out of the shop excited, proud, maybe happy. Months ago I had anxiety attacks over ordering coffee. Now I look at hands holding a brown paper bag, like a school lunch. It's just weed.

I stand outside a train station, the blare of the city in my ears. Anonymous. I bring a pen to my cold lips, breath condensing in the winter air. He said to draw until it burns,

15

for the first time. A white, circular light. It vanishes. I collapse onto a wall, coughing out a lung. *Holy shit, fuck.* I feel bile on my lips. Everything burns. Then, weightlessness; my head is heavy with nothing. I slide down the wall, sitting on the freezing pavement, legs pulled up to my chest. I laugh. *Fucking hell.* Discomfort vanishes. I feel fake, inhuman, absent. I laugh. Stumbling through the station, somehow, I laugh. Boarding a train, filled to the brim, somehow, I laugh. I find my seat, somehow. Eyes dancing, alive with grand humor, a hidden joke: *They don't know I'm high.* I laugh.

He says weed is not addictive. Ryan told him that when he hit a bong for the first time in a musty basement that felt like a crypt. He remembers how the hit burned blisters in his throat, the tang of the icy lemon popsicle that he desperately sucked the lifeblood out of to get any relief. He remembers how he wrapped his mouth around the bong, the curiosity of what another might feel like, what another strain of bud might taste of, whether the high would be a cozy fire on a winter's night or the biting warmth of sunlight. He dropped out of college in his sophomore year after Ryan told him about the smoke shop, about how he samples every product, and then the ache of discovery made home in his chest. He works a shift with a different puff bar in his hand, every hour, a different rig, cart, expertly feeling out the consistency of the smoke that swirls through his mouth, relishing the overwhelming strawberry, pineapple, vanilla. Each day a new product, endless to uncover. A scientist in the field, a polar expedition where there's always another glacier, another species of penguin to find, another aurora that shocks the mind; tantalizing, enrapturing. It's not addictive, of course. Ryan told him so.

I wait in a crowded dispensary, med card in my hands. Tired. A man banters with an attendant: *I just got my paycheck and came right here. I can't live without this stuff.* They both laughed. I think about an appointment, an assistant telling me to check a box; I apparently have chronic nerve pain. The doctor agreed after a thorough examination through a screen. It's my turn. The budtender smiles at me. She recommends a sour diesel cart, whatever that means. It's my first time, they give me a discount, a free battery. Now I just inhale, no buttons, no clicking. I pay with cash, a Christmas gift from my grandparents. A deep pain squirms in my chest. I walk out, eyes haggard, exhausted.

I sit in some kid's basement, staring at a wall. Weed of course, alcohol, Adderall. Music blares. I see shadows dancing in the light of orange LEDs. The wall is concrete, decorated with pipes. A good wall, a fine wall, strong. I blink. A twitch that courses through my whole body, an electric shock. Everything soars into my mind all at once, the music, the lights, the people. I lean over, shuddering, overwhelmed. *What. The. Fuck.* I feel my breath quickening, psychotic panic terrorizing my mind. I look up. What a wall, fine, strong. I wonder if I can be content, happy. I blink. *What. The. Fuck.* I blink. Standing up, finally, stumbling over to a group that looks like my friends. They stare, laughing. I can barely hear. Everything is blurry. I struggle to decipher what might be speech. *You are so fucked up. Go lie down.* I find myself in a seat, staring at a wall, fine, strong, decorated with pipes.

My friends say weed is not addictive. Oh, they smoke socially of course. At every shitty party where we would drink summer-warm Bud Light and play beer pong with those red cups filled with thin blades of grass and some foul-smelling brown liquid—just down a driveway, lying against the back of an old Mazda, you'd find a solitary circle, orange flame flashing, the beacon of a lighthouse. A pipe would change hands, every hit dirtying the glass, the remnants of burnt flower scarring the green bowl. I'd always sit and lean against raw car, muffler poking into my back, and just watch. One hit turned into two, into three; then edibles, ten milligrams suddenly fifty; a six-second draw to a desperate sucking, a baby studiously at work on their pacifier, until the light of a pen blinked in danger and they'd suddenly release, crumbling to the floor, a rush of coughs mingling with sharp laughter. There was weed with acid. With nic. With Adderall, with alcohol. A veneer of afternoon sunlight that painted the background of experience, a simple warmth of reassurance. It's only at parties, though. You might find one, or two, or all, smoking in the small of their rooms, in dark nights staring at the light of a monitor that made eyes squint and cower, where the light of a pen found like company.

I'm draped across a bed, unclean. A battered pen—chipped paint, stained with beer—in my hands, against my dry lips. A light in the darkness, of salvation, terror.

A halo, the white of an angel. Draw until it burns. I fall over, coughing out a lung. Adrenaline, panic. Cloudy, weightless, panic. I roll over. *What?* My breath quickens. My meds, SSRI. Serotonin. Weed produces serotonin. I shiver, a cold sweat. Unbearable heat. I tear off my clothes, cover myself with a blanket. My phone in a shaking hand, reading stories of seizures, paralysis, death. *I'm dying. Of serotonin syndrome.* A twitch shocks my body. *Do I call an ambulance, call my mom?* A shiver. *You wanted this. You've been searching for this. You're a coward, you couldn't do it. Now you have it. You want it, right? Lie still. That's right.* I close eyes burned red. *Let it be quick.*

The day after I died I told my therapist weed is not addictive. Late December sunlight filtered through wide windows to illuminate the despair in her eyes. *Evan, this is serious. You've smoked every day since October?* I've forgotten her name. *Look, I know good people in an outpatient substance abuse program. I can put you in contact with them today.* Substance abuse? What? *You need to stop smoking.* I felt a little annoyed, then a little angry, then fucking furious. *I* need to stop smoking? What the fuck, smoking was the only thing keeping me alive, didn't she understand that? That I did all the right things, took all of their medications, even when they placed me over a midnight cold toilet, bile an icicle from my lips. When they made me forget a day, a month, a year, and numb, so oppressively numb. That I went to therapy and confessed the worms that squirm in my head even though the acknowledgment made them feast on my brain. That I did everything they asked and was still spiraling. And so, one of *them*, one of those useless therapists, psychiatrists, whatever, was telling me to never relax, never find any relief, to stop feeling that little bit of happiness, all that was left? Aren't they supposed to care, why aren't they helping, why do they want to hurt me? *No, I'm fine. I'll survive, and I can stop whenever I want. It's not addictive.* Oh, those eyes. I rose like an old man from that clothy blue couch and hugged her as I left. She asked me to. I'm not sure I would have if she hadn't.

"The image of smoke expelling from my mouth, myself seated at my desk, the smoke blown into my bookshelf and window. The smoke mingles with the sunlight, twisting behind a shelf that holds my dreams, my life. Beauty, I think."

I look up from my journal, to that vanishing smoke. Precariously perched on those miserable shit-brown chairs that poke the lower back—I am high. I have been for three days. I mean been back for three days. My roommates, they look at me differently. Judging. They're loud, the bright lights from their paradise pinning me against the wall, some wanton criminal in a 1940s cartoon, some stage attraction that all might laugh at. I ran out of bud last night, walking in that freezing January night with a joint, sitting on a street corner as ash built up on the ground. I remember how the roach tumbled down a wet drain, light bouncing back and forth and back and forth. I remember how I lay in my bed violently twitching, glad the overwhelming panic that killed me might provide voracious

distraction. I went to class, earlier, smoking over coffee. Gothic literature. I loved it, loved that I was finally learning something that moved me, that matched the despair that I was obsessed with surrounding me, something that made me actually feel. Well, would have if I wasn't so high, I hope. The cart is starting to taste like metal. Every hit makes me gag from the tang, makes me feel as if I'm pumping poison into my body, my blood, a little stream of silver swimming through a corpse. My lungs feel tight, out of breath always. They hurt in the best way.

I sit in an already warm leather armchair across from one of those psychiatrists whose eyes were bright and welcoming. One who, after I shared that I was sensitive to light, would dim the room to a welcoming warmth that I might fully open squinted eyes. I told him. Routine, now. I always felt a little eager to share my misery, to have someone nod and admit that what had happened was quite tragic and I was indeed unlucky and completely justified in being an addict. A what? I shivered in delight at the words of a child that all might bow before. *I'm sorry.* He adjusted my medication, promising that it would get better, that it would be hard and I needed to wait. To survive. Whatever. And then that miserable mantra, one that rings in the ears after every appointment. *You need to stop smoking.*

I perform before an audience of ghosts. I'm leaving today, after I stumbled around with music blaring in my ears, breath heavy through a mask, unaware that I was having a panic attack until I stepped into my dorm. After I woke up and couldn't move, limbs lead, utterly dead. After the mere thought of entering a dining hall, being observed, made me want to reopen scars on my wrists. Violin chords echo through a lecture hall, abandoned on an early Saturday morning, rows and rows of seats empty, all fixated on the child before them. I play Bach, his Chaconne in D minor. An invisible performance, the only one I could ever want. A flourish of the bow, that last D vibrating the air of a grand theater. I set down my work of wood, smiling in pleasure at the simple perfection of music, the way it scratches the brain. An abyssal trek to a nearby chair covered with icy sunlight and I lie down, my head against the desk, cool wood prickling my cheek. I quietly sob, for the first time. *What am I going to do? How can I live like this? Why am I a failure? What did I do wrong?* My pen out of a pocket, a hit, metal in my mouth. I feel nothing. A hit as I wait on a train platform, the majestic blue gray of an Amtrak machine blurring past. It hurts. A hit as I turn a corner on a city street, bright spectrums of light dancing in the night. My mom's car, a wordless drive home.

An armchair. New medication. *You need to stop smoking.*

Every night at eleven my phone would violently vibrate to tell me I'm an addict. It was some stupid app that I installed in a moment of guilt, when I'd lock my pen away and swear off bud, where I'd assure my sobbing mother whose tears stained a stinking, weeks old sweatshirt that, yes, I had stopped smoking. The new meds hurt. Abilify gave me a never-ending prickling throughout my body, my feet, hands, so

bad it made me bite flesh to make it stop, make it stop, the pain, it hurts, move, do something, please, make it stop. Racing to the smoke shop, moaning, begging for a cart after being sober for a week. They took me off Sertraline and I almost died, waking up a monster, a tyranny that made a mountain summit out of the bathroom and placed unbearable weights on blistering lips. I wished I could leave the world. I was horrified that the only way to leave is to die. Those late-night highs felt shitty, incomplete, a facsimile. Shadows would dance amidst soft candlelight as I opened that little black box to forage for the pen, a treasure trove filled with empty carts, hemp rolling papers, green-blue pipes, half-empty grinders—my shaking hands probing through that filthy mess. They barely worked, the carts, amidst guilt. That right after I took a hit, I'd open a phone, eyes terrorized by the bright, and find that app; that I'd reset a daylong streak and admit I couldn't stay sober.

A new diagnosis. F1x—substance abuse disorder. *You need to stop smoking.*

A night, one of hundreds. Assailed by the light of a monitor. I stare at a mountain village in fierce battle with a blizzard, wishing intently, with the whole of my mind, to simply be transported to that paradise, anywhere, just away. I'm not here, I'm above, watching myself stare into that horrible light; watching myself sit at dinner and remember nothing, watching myself wake and sleep over and over again until every moment is one of misery. I can't focus, my thoughts mud—like slime that drips through my skull. I want it to just end, to be over. I take a hit.

Another. I'm still watching myself. Nothing. Shivering, clawing at my face, my eyes, trying to hurt, to feel pain. Why isn't it working, it's supposed to feel good and warm and a blanket and in my head and calm me and I should forget why can't I forget.

It doesn't work anymore.

Evan, you should be proud of yourself. Two months sober is amazing. You're finally starting to improve.

I wait outside a smoke shop, "21 and older" decal hanging over me like a cross. *Why do I have to do this? I'm fine?* I leave today, I need it now. Inside, they've renovated, expanded, yet still those same disposables, rigs, vaporizers. I walk up to the counter and smile at the cashier, the one from that bygone era, with that horrible goatee and slicked back dark hair, smile as he recognizes me, as we banter about a different cart, debate a new brand of edibles, yet my limbs still shake as I pay with cash I stole from my parents. *Oh, you're going to love those edibles, I'm absolutely addicted to them.* I glance up at him from my wallet. It's a little ironic. *Me too.*

I walk outside with a grin on my face, shame vanishing. I look at hands holding a brown paper bag, like a school lunch. It's just weed.

Glossary

Abilify, antipsychotic drug
Adderall, medication for ADHD
boba, tapioca pearls in bubble tea
bong, water pipe
bud, portion of cannabis plant
budtender, sales clerk in vape store
cart and battery, vape pen
clover, cannabis
edibles, food forms of cannabis
[a] plug, dealer
puff bar, disposable vaping device
rig, pipe or other device for smoking cannabis
sour diesel cart, cartridge for hybrid strain of cannabis
SSRI, selective serotonin reuptake inhibitor

John Wall Barger

The Effluvial Redemption of Samuel Sewall

Samuel Sewall, a judge at the 1692 Salem witchcraft trials,
killed women. Sewage—from Old French *essouier*,
      "to drain"—released to waterways

    such as rivers flowing to larger bodies like seas.
A ghoulish, fire-breathing judge.
      In a sedimentation tank,

    fecal sludge is pumped, bacteria
dried, detoxified. Processed, treated,
      purified. Sewall, in puritanical plumage,

    fluent in the ruinous vernacular,
condemned twenty to death by hanging.
      Any remaining organic material

    dissolves in the effluent. Five years later
Sewall repented, admitting
      he was wrong. Which is called humus.

    In 1718, he was appointed chief justice,
superior court of judicature.
      In these tanks, solids sink

    to the bottom. In his old age, he criticized slavery.
These Ethiopians, he wrote,
      ought to be treated

with a Respect agreeable.
Sewage can be used to run your car,
            make methane, hydroelectric power,

coal. World history a draining.
So then, says the Son of Man,
            because thou art lukewarm,

and neither cold nor hot, I will spue thee
out of my mouth. An eruption,
            regurgitation. It can even power

cell phones. A flood. Sewall
considered himself more at fault than others.
            Fecal bacteria

may occur in ambient water
as a result of the overflow of domestic sewage.
            No other judge

had a change of heart.
Trace amounts of feces exist in all water
            on earth.

R. S. Powers

Everyone I Know Is a Terrible Person

I'D BEEN AT DREAMBOAT English for maybe a half-year on a really bad two-year contract when I was named King Teacher. This was in Beijing, a few summers before the 2008 Olympics, when it was easier for a nobody to find their way into the country. They'd already named Mr. Clean as the new King, but then something apparently went wrong with the business license and police started doing visa checks, and Mr. Clean left and panic spread since all foreign teachers lived in the same high-rise. When the air was good, I could see out my window from some twenty stories up, the new subway line being built all day and night. The tourist-visa hires pulled runners to avoid deportation. Threats were made to keep the passports of all work-visa hires in a safe so we too wouldn't leave, then our monthly pay was cut (to help fix the apparent license problem), so everyone else fled except for Mr. Lies, Ms. Porn, and me—Mr. Loser. Rumor was the police were looking for someone. Meanwhile, I thought I was in love.

I was also still religiously googling my new legal name and was no longer in touch with anyone back home, and starting to think my few years away from undergrad would become a decade. When I could find sleep I'd get stuck in sci-fi dreams about a bright orange sandstorm that would slowly bury me along with the capital's fifteen-plus million people.

★

I WAS THRILLED ABOUT my sudden coronation.

Mrs. Many-Audis, Dreamboat's founder, who dressed like she ran a Fortune 500 company, with a bouffant like a lion's mane, had her two young overworked assistants, Mr. Overly-Fluent and Ms. Overly-Qualified, bring me down one floor to her smoky office at midnight, six hours before I had to catch a charter bus for my newest teaching assignment on a far-flung campus that during the seventies had been a cement brickmaking commune.

From behind her faux-marble desk she told me, through Mr. Overly-Fluent, why Mr. Serious-Anger-Issues, Dreamboat's first hire and original King Teacher (a title I'd learn was his idea), was returning to Arizona. Something about how the ear acupuncture he'd been doing to treat his increasingly morbid weight problem wasn't working. In the resignation email they showed me, he'd also provided a more typical lie: a mess of relatives back home had "stage-five" brain cancer.

She saw my smirk and assured me, through Mr. Overly-Fluent: His exodus lacks relevance to our constabulary entanglement. Don't worry, be happy. The show must go on.

In a few days, I'd run an orientation for at least a dozen new tourist-visa hires, giving the same spiel that had promised me flexible hours, airfare reimbursement, and more. And I'd cover Mr. Serious-Anger-Issues's section at the far-flung dusty campus the next morning, meaning another twenty high schoolers would be in my sunny classroom with a broken AC unit. I'd get a new business card and have my photo featured on a website they were building. Did I know anything about web design? Could I complete a website someone else started?

No no, no-no-no, I said about the website.

Are you excited? Mrs. Many-Audis beamed in sudden English.

I don't know what to say, I said.

Congratulations, Mr. Overly-Fluent said, standing to shake my hand.

You'll do very well, Ms. Overly-Qualified said, giving me a thumbs up.

Xiè-xiè, I said, in my awful Chinese. Thank you. But why me?

I didn't mean to ask that. It just came out.

I mean I'm glad, I said, honored. You won't regret it.

Mr. Overly-Fluent translated, and everyone returned to their smiling.

You are not our primary choice, Mrs. Many-Audis said, through Mr. Overly-Fluent, but you are the most incomparable choice. She ended the meeting by reciting Dreamboat's slogan: Are you ready to revolutionize education?

Yes, I said. Yes.

★

THEY KNEW I WAS a terrible teacher. I didn't plan. I overslept. Nothing would've made Mr. Lies happier than being made a King of something. I knew he'd flip out about not getting the job.

Ms. Porn should've gotten it. Before I left my room for my coronation, she was half looking online for a new teaching gig she said would take us to a new part of China, and half composing her version of a resignation email—Are you Catholic? she said. She was on her laptop in my bed.

No, I said, washing my face.

So it would be weird, she said, if I wrote we're taking a sabbatical to go on the Way of Saint James pilgrimage?

They were lucky to have her. She grew up in a not-nice (her words) trailer park, in a part of Michigan indistinguishable from Siberia (also her words), to parents that threw plates at one another even after signing divorce papers in the parking lot of her high school graduation. She told me it was always left to her to change the diapers of her big and simple (her words again) half-brother ten years her senior, and still she won a full ride to a big state school, finishing with degrees in literature and Spanish with a minor in philosophy. I told her I'd never heard her speak Spanish so she threw off the comforter, model-walked to the desk, downloaded her twenty-page honors thesis (written in Spanish!), and read from it as she paced my room in the nude.

When I returned after my coronation, the lights were out and she was asleep. The air was particularly bad, so my view toward the heart of Beijing was an ashen void punctuated by the dull-orange specters of nearby streetlights. I undressed and slipped into bed.

They fire you before you could quit? she mumbled into her pillow.

They told me why Anger-Issues left, I said. They made me King.

You won the booby prize? she said, her eyes still closed.

It's going to be a lot of work, I said, but I think I'm ready.

I wanted her to be proud of me.

Aye aye, Mr. King-Loser-Booby-Prize, she said, turned over, and fell asleep again.

★

IT WAS HER IDEA to give everyone at Dreamboat nicknames only we knew. I was her Mr. Lovable-Loser after drunkenly proclaiming at an expat bar that only losers end up in China teaching English, which became Mr. Loser after I kept losing my passport whenever the police showed up to do their check. While the two bored-looking young female cops watched me rifle through piles of clothes and messy drawers, she'd stand in my doorframe and barely contain her laughter. She was already almost fluent so I could only guess at what she was telling them.

★

THE NEXT MORNING on the charter bus it was still dark. Everyone, even the driver, seemed asleep. I texted Ms. Porn: Zoo to celebrate new job after I teach?

We'd been talking about going for ages. We could go and I could tell her what happened to me back home. I wanted to start talking to her about spending our lives together.

What Mr. Clean might've done as head teacher was also on my mind. He'd always received glowing feedback from his students, which we'd get to read in the mass evaluation emails. The best scores meant a cash bonus, so no one liked him. He'd come up when we were in my apartment drinking after teaching. Mr. Thinks-He's-Hemingway said he had the creepiest smile in the universe. Ms. Divorced-Florida-Cheats-On-Racist-Welsh-Boif said she observed his class and he was terrible. Ms. Montenegro-Pretending-To-Be-Canadian said she was allergic to his rancid cologne. Mr. Racist-Welsh-Cuckold said he'd put money on him sleeping with his students. Ms. Porn said to put a gun in her mouth if she ever ended up like him.

I knew Mr. Clean as misunderstood. He was the only one I ever told that I'd changed my name. He was almost fifty, tanned-white, clean-shaven, and completely bald—exactly the chemical company mascot you're picturing. He had a dull stud in his left ear, wore tight black jeans, red leather shoes with no socks, monocolor T-shirts that emphasized his flabby biceps. He was always smiling and told people he spent decades bouncing around Southeast Asia. He and I taught next-door to one another on my first teaching assignment—four sessions at a summer camp for middle schoolers: eight days on from seven a.m. to seven p.m. with an hour-long packed, city bus trip to and from the camp's secluded leafy grounds, then two days off spent sleeping or outside day-drinking at the cheap Sichuan restaurant across the street from our high-rise.

You ever try to kill yourself? was how he got the conversation started.

I was trying to feed the stray yellow Pekinese we called "mǎ-ma-hū-hū" (Chinese for "so-so") bits of my mapo tofu from a broad spoon. He was pouring me my third or fourth Tsingtao tall boy. What kinda fucked up . . . ? I said, scrunching my face.

Hey, he said, holding up his hands, still lightly smiling, I've been watching you. You don't seem happy. He asked me where I was from. What my parents were like. Where I went to school. What goals I had. What brought me to China. About me and Ms. Porn.

You want the truth? I said, adding: I shouldn't say this.

My lips are sealed, he said.

She has this middle school friend, I said, a guy with a potbelly, who's twice now mailed her care packages, like she's at summer camp.

So? he said. That's quite sweet.

I said this guy included handwritten letters about visiting her dad and mom and half-brother, and sent things like small boxes of sugary cereal, Midwestern cheese things, and dozens of burned DVDs of porn with labels like "quicksand" and "lesbian party hat" and "dorm rooms." I made sure no one we knew was nearby. She won't let me watch them, I said. She sends him things like Chinese coins and her own handwritten letters she won't let me read.

Yeah, you shouldn't have told me that, he said.

We kept drinking.

But everyone has secrets, he said. Stuff they're running away from.

He looked at me like he wanted to tell me something.

What *really* brought you here? he said, still smiling. And don't give me any of that seeking adventure or transformative new experiences bullshit. He laughed and clapped me on the back: You're not *really* from Maine, are you?

★

I GOT AS FAR as it being my parents' idea to legally change my first and last names. They'd read an article about how "the dark web never forgets" and the asshole lawyer they hired wholeheartedly agreed and I went along with everything.

I'd become infamous on campus when an article about the lawsuit my ex's parents filed against me, written by an aspiring journalist on my dorm floor, appeared on the student newspaper's website and was shared and shared and shared online.

My business ethics professor was the first to pull me aside to ask if it was me in the article after his several-hundred-student lecture. A few national papers picked up the story and one used my name. Out of the blue, the student newspaper editor called me on my dorm phone to apologize for printing my name, but that didn't stop the emails and voice mails. My dormmate, my best friend at school, put in for a room transfer. He said I was a monster. I stopped going to class and moved back home. My therapist told me to stop googling myself, that my life wasn't over. The lawsuit was tossed and the plan was I'd transfer to another school. My parents kept asking if I'd have to register as a sex offender and the asshole lawyer kept assuring them I didn't. Future employers, my parents kept saying, your future wife, they won't know.

And then I didn't get into another Ivy. My parents said no to teaching abroad before saying I'd make a great teacher. I'd reapply for school when I was ready.

★

Bᴜᴛ I ᴅᴏᴜʙᴛ Mr. Clean could even follow what had come out of me. He also probably thought I was hung up on something that was actually nothing. It wasn't like I committed a crime, right? Everyone's unlucky, he said, biting into a roast sparrow on a skewer.

Not everyone, I said.

You're young, he said, chewing. Be who you need to be.

★

Wʜɪʟᴇ ᴍʏ sᴛᴜᴅᴇɴᴛs ᴡᴏʀᴋᴇᴅ on speeches for an upcoming competition, I sat at the teacher's computer looking through new-hire resumes and headshots—young and middle-aged white Americans; none from where I was from. An email from Ms. Porn arrived.

She was being put on a train early the next morning to teach at a four-week summer camp in Inner Mongolia. Never-ending grasslands, she wrote, fermented mare's milk, the angry ghosts of Genghis Khan. . . . It'll be beautiful. They're giving me a bonus to go.

She'd asked if I could come, but the word was no: You'll be oh so busy as reigning King.

Zoo? I wrote back.

Let's zoo it up, came the quick reply. Btw have ridic gossip about Mr. Clean.

Not many wanted to practice their speeches when they were finished writing. One was a strident young woman who considered the death of her mother from brain cancer to be an opportunity to overcome adversity. One was a quiet young man who laid out a fairly researched case for why Osama bin Laden should be considered a folk hero. One was a confident young man who spoke with extraordinary eloquence on the need for radical reform in the Chinese public education system. I found

myself standing to applaud when he finished only to find everyone looking at me strangely. When no one else wanted to speak, I opened up the class for questions about America, but instead most wanted to know about my work contract. I was giggling, trying to explain my new job title, when a thickly bespectacled and heavily pimpled new student who came to class with his own name tag ("Peter!") raised his hand.

Teacher, he said with obvious sympathy, they are clearly cheating you.

I let everyone go at least fifteen minutes early.

Waiting for the return bus, I spent lunch and the rest of the early hot afternoon under a weeping willow overlooking an opaquely green man-made lake full of hungry koi. Students eventually would show me the photos they took of me sleeping in the shade. One used Photoshop to add rainbow text of something I once said in class: Be who you need to be.

Boarding the bus, I texted Ms. Porn: We don't belong anywhere, but we have each other.

Halfway back, she hadn't replied. I added: I won't stop missing you.

★

Sʜᴇ ᴀɴᴅ I sat in the shade of a gift shop looking out at a zebra family lazing in mild sunshine. The crowds were preposterous, and every so often a mother would approach and position their young child on the bench beside us so they could take photos of them meeting foreigners. Most of the kids tried to ask us questions in English. The few who cried and called for their mothers aiming cameras, Ms. Porn explained, thought they were being given away.

You're lying, I said.

I swear to Cthulhu themself, she said.

I told her my parents in their last email

27

mentioned visiting. Maybe they'll be here when you get back? They'll think you're hilarious. My mom speaks a little Spanish.

You're so lucky, she said, to have parents who love you.

You don't actually think that? I said.

Did you tell them we're together?

No, I said.

All she wanted to talk about was what she'd heard at brunch about Mr. Clean. After getting her Inner Mongolia assignment she met up with a gaggle of tourist-visa hires who'd fled Dreamboat. All already had found better-paying jobs at other teaching companies.

Mr. Clean's literally a pedophile, Ms. Porn said.

She said Mr. Thinks-He's-Hemingway ran into Mr. Clean at an interview for a kindergarten job. Mr. Thinks-He's-Hendrix saw him in a swanky part of the central business district. But it was Ms. Covert-Mormon-Missionary who said she heard from Mr. Lies that the police started snooping around Dreamboat because Mr. Clean kept giving out his cell phone number to the kids he was teaching. He was texting them about sex, Ms. Porn said, and he was showing people their texts. He was bragging about it! He did this while teaching kids!

This is from Mr. Lies? I said.

I know, but Ms. Missionary said it was the only sense he'd ever made, Ms. Porn said. Didn't you work with him at a summer camp?

Mr. Lies? I said.

No, Mr. Clean, she said. Now maybe Mr. Toucher?

Yeah, on my first job.

Did he ever show you any of the texts?

I guess not, I said.

★

I GAVE OUT MY CELL phone number on my first job. All the other teachers warned me: They'll ask you, but don't do it. They'll text. I went to write my name on the board and the two dozen eight- to thirteen-year-olds got up and swarmed me. Please, they kept saying in English. We'll sit when you give us your number. I relented and they whipped out their phones. That morning, I taught them the words to John Lennon's "Imagine" and we sang along. During lunch, a number texted me: Teacher do you know what is fuck? I showed the text to my Chinese co-teacher, the director of the camp, and I told Mr. Overly-Fluent. I never gave out my number again.

But I didn't tell her any of this.

I should've gotten us out of the ticket line and found a spot where we wouldn't be bothered so I could tell her that the last time I was on my own in the shabby law offices of the asshole lawyer my parents wouldn't fire, he told me I should write a memoir.

Those things sell, he said with apparent cheer. You still have tuition bills.

She'd been so open to me about her abusive exes, and I hadn't told her I was a shy virgin hideously out of my element when I started college, that there was this girl at the end of my dorm floor also out of her element. She was a sophomore, a newly decided art design major, a brain cancer survivor since middle school, and a recent sorority exile. She wore a Rachel-from-*Friends* blond wig since she couldn't grow a lot of hair and she wanted to hide the shunt running down her neck under the skin that continued to drain fluid from her brain into her stomach.

She and I bonded over a mutual disdain for one of her three roommates, a gothy music major who wouldn't stop joking about having a threesome with us. I keep finding her bloody lipstick, she said, on everything in our fridge! It was noon the first time we got naked, so we closed all the blinds in her dorm room and put the dead bolt on. She asked me to help her look inside herself with a mirror. She told me she'd never seen. We started saying we loved one another and I have no idea why. She wanted to video the role-play she liked, which I didn't want to do, but she told me she'd never seen herself having sex. She was very loud, and given what we were saying to one another, I don't know why one of us didn't think about a hotel.

What happened over the next few months was a bit of a dumb blur.

The RA on my floor, a psychology master's student, got to me first about the noise complaints, and I let loose in her room about the many video files on my girlfriend's laptop. She asked if I wanted to file a complaint and I said yes and my girlfriend wound up before a review board that told her she might have to live off-campus, that she could end up with a criminal record. She found me in my dorm room afterward. I told her it was a mistake, that I still loved her. I'd find out she then told her roommates I liked to beat her and one filed a complaint and I was brought in before a review board. We were both told to stay away from one another. And I still don't know how the one video ended up online. My parents wanted me to say it was her who did it. I was walking to class one morning when two muscly frat pledges pointed at me: It's rape face! Rape face! In the video, she's on top of me and I'm half-choking her and she's saying: Show me your rape face. She

attempted suicide in one of the showers on our floor and one of her roommates said it was my fault. Her parents sued me and the school. At one of the depositions, her parents and mine were in the room when I was asked to describe her and my sexual fantasies.

Before I left the country—and I've never told anyone this—I was in the habit of searching for the video on porn sites and emailing their admins to take it down.

★

WE WERE STILL in line and all I managed to say was something about an ex's suicide attempt. Ms. Porn told me how one of her best friends from high school went out into the tundra, without telling anyone, to kill himself with a shotgun after four straight years of not making the jazz band. His fingers, she said, holding my hands, were too stubby for the sax.

Why did you come to China? I said weakly.

Fucking adventure, she said. New experiences. I had to make sure the world wasn't flat.

She must've known I'd fallen for her. She knew me.

But there was no way she could've known I thought she'd saved my life.

Later, on the elevator ride up to my floor, she sang a slow waltzing version of "It's a Small World" while hugging me and I felt my heart exploding into her chest. At my window, the air crystal clear, I pointed and said we could see the shadowy outlines of distant mountains. No, we can't, she said, looking up at me. She had big milk-blue eyes, like ancient glaciers. She took my left hand and put it on her left breast. She'd taken off her bra. I told her to take off her T-shirt and she did. I told her to take off her jean shorts and she slid

29

everything to the cold tile. She kept on her neon-yellow socks. She pushed me backward onto the bed and undid my belt and ripped my teaching pants and boxers to my knees. Just like in the video with my ex, when she was on top of me, eyes closed, hips grinding, she had to hold her mouth with both hands.

Before falling asleep late, we tried imagining out loud what our futures in China might look like. Whatever awful things you've done, she said, her head on my chest hair, Dreamboat doesn't deserve you. Whatever you think you're doing, get out before it's too late.

I can't for the life of me remember what she said her plans were.

★

WE WOKE AFTER a few hours to her cell phone ringing. My phone was on silent and Mr. Overly-Fluent was looking for me. Mr. Lies was a mess and I needed to help.

Stay, Ms. Porn said, reaching for me.

I'm King, I said.

Mr. Lies's first-floor door was wide open. His face leaking blood, he was on the floor slurring incoherently. Ms. Overly-Qualified and several new male hires I didn't know were wrestling with his limbs. The goal was to get him in a taxi and to a hospital. Something about pills and booze. Ms. Porn's original nickname for Mr. Lies went something like Mr. Son-of-a-Bowling-Ball-and-a-Bridge-Troll, but eventually she had to agree the name was too much. When I first met him, I was in the main office waiting to do a demo lesson. He made a beeline through the door and around the conference table to sit across from me. He was at least middle-aged, squat, round, and brooding. He had blotchy skin and white flakes throughout his thin M of red

hair, in his sideburns, and on his tweed sport coat. You the judge, sport? he said, glaring.

Mr. Overly-Fluent was in the kitchen slowly smoking a cigarette. This consultancy lifestyle is a bit Sisyphean, he said. Don't you think?

What happened? I said.

This Don Quixote came to the Middle Kingdom to escape inescapable demons.

Outside, I helped flag a taxi. Limp Mr. Lies was maneuvered into the front seat. The car sped off with everyone inside except me and Mr. Overly-Fluent.

You go sleep, he said, hailing another. Tomorrow is the big show.

I couldn't help but think he was testing me.

What happens when he gets fired? I said.

Fired? Mr. Overly-Fluent laughed. We are commodities. He has use when sober.

He wants my job, I said.

No shit, he said.

He lies about me, I said. Big evil lies. What should I do?

Mr. Overly-Fluent stomped out his dying cigarette.

Everyone you know is a terrible person, he said. Be who you need to be.

Ms. Porn was dead asleep when I returned to my room. When I woke the next morning, she was gone. Everything outside, as far out into the city as I could see, was coated in a thin layer of bright-orange powder. A quick sandstorm had swept in around dawn.

★

TO PREPARE FOR the new-teacher orientation, I wrote down a list of the fake perks the company sold me on. I also wrote new-hire nicknames I'd send Ms. Porn: Mr. Stolen-Valor (or Mr. Alien-vs-Predator-

Neck-Tattoo), Mrs. Tinkerbell (a middle-aged woman whose Hotmail email was glitterkitty69), and Mr. Quasimodo (a six-foot-six former prison guard).

You're my Queen, I wrote. All hail us!

After a week, she emailed me about her new boyfriend, a tall albino Irish guy, another teacher at the camp. She wrote he could play every Britney Spears song on his acoustic guitar, and she attached a video of them singing an upbeat duet of "I'm a Slave 4 U" to a packed auditorium, at least a thousand kids clapping along as best they could.

In her last email, the camp had been over for weeks and she and Mr. Britney-Spears were touring a part of China bordering North Korea. She attached photos of them at the remains of a train bridge bombed by the US in the 1950s. She said she hoped to see me whenever she got back to Beijing. She had a bottle of North Korean wine with my name on it.

I never saw her again.

★

TO BE HONEST, I don't tell anyone who really knows me this story.

I threw myself into the job, became quite good at it, convinced Mrs. Many-Audis to make new business cards that read "Head Teacher." When they were delivered, Mr. Overly-Fluent burst out laughing: The guillotined educator! Mr. Lies demanded to be named Chief Teacher and stayed on as long as I did. Dreamboat shuttered when Mrs. Many-Audis's husband was jailed over an illegal real estate project he spearheaded. The website stayed up for years before disappearing. I last saw Mr. Clean from afar in a thrumming dance club.

He was wearing a glittering black T-shirt and black pants. He was dancing up in the middle of the main stage. His eyes were closed, arms held aloft, hands writhing. Surrounded by young male expats, he looked like the happiest person in existence.

I'm married, and you don't need to know anything about my wife. Mr. Overly-Fluent and I started a teaching company. He was a tank driver in the army and is an amazing manager. We've garnered major connections—I was recently flown back to Beijing by the Ministry of Health to do a crash course on cocktail conversation for high-ranking doctors headed overseas. Many worked in big hospitals during SARS. They have stories they can't tell anyone. . . .

★

I LIED, JUST NOW.

Before I left Beijing for a teaching job in Gansu Province, off toward Central Asia, she was in all these subway ads for one of the best business English schools in China. In the ad, she was in a blue power suit, her posture bolt-straight. She looked like a politician but she hated politicians. She was smiling wider than I'd ever seen her smile, standing next to a young Chinese man in a black suit, the two of them against a blue background, each of them holding up one wrist, a thick rope binding their wrists together. The slogan at the bottom read "hand in hand we grow." I saw the exact same ad maybe thousands of times. I kept waiting to run into her.

I still google her, but nothing comes up.

Her name is Angelika, but she preferred Leeka, said she was never meant to be an angel. Can't pick who we were, she once told me over beers, but we can pick who we will be.

If you need to know: my name is Peter.

Michael Hettich

Impressions and Collage: A Memoir in Glimpses

What is it that lives in the past and longs for the future, or lives in the future and longs for the past?
—Mark Strand

1.

I'M IN OUR NEIGHBORHOOD park watching a young woman at play with her baby. It's a spring afternoon. They are laughing at nothing, simply laughing at their own happiness. There are pigeons and older children, people reading off phones; a group of girls in the distance is dancing and laughing to a pop tune of many years ago. The grass is soggy and the day is growing cool. Now the woman picks up her little boy and starts to walk slowly home, carrying him all the way. I imagine she loves the weight of him, the sweet smell of his breath. She sings silly songs as they walk along, and he sings back, still laughing, still too young to form the words, though he appears to understand them all. They stop often to admire flowers and insects and pieces of glass, newspapers blowing down the street, bikes passing on the sidewalk.

I imagine someone watches from an upstairs window, a lonely man who lives in a wheelchair.

Somehow, without knowing it, they bless him as they pass.

IN ANOTHER ROOM, a young man has been praying for hours, quietly rocking back and forth on his knees, whispering a little without words, like the breath of wind beneath a slightly open window. He's dressed neatly, a dress shirt tucked in his jeans; his shoes wait at the door. He prays for a glimpse of something he finds difficult to name. None of his many friends knows he does this; his family has no inkling. But he prays for longer and longer periods every day, until he's almost disappeared. He doesn't believe in any god, as far as he knows; he just knows that by praying he reaches something true. And it's not like meditation, since he feels as though he's thinking while he prays: thinking of the birds that fly into windows; of dogs caught in the middle of highways; of children lost in crowds, lost at a border, lost and abandoned. He's thinking of the people who have learned how to lie so well they can't tell what truth is anymore. He's an ordinary young man, a regular guy. He wants to get married someday and have children. When he finally stops praying, he steps out into the bustling afternoon and sees the woman and her boy bopping happily along the sidewalk toward home; he stands and watches them as the dusk-light settles into evening.

2.

OUR LIVES ARE SUPERIMPOSED over each other—another and another and so on, each of the superimposed lives unaware of the others lying across it like translucent tracing paper, palimpsest or stained glass windows. A woman imagines walking all day along an old carriage road in the woods, dusky even at noon, then stepping out into sunlight and watching dragonflies rise up and hover over the long grasses buzzing with bees, walking into that field, still squinting from the darkness, thinking of her parents and their parents and their parents' parents, as far back as math might take her, which is thousands of years, to realize each of these lives is living still, in her movements and gestures, the way she tosses her hair, her habit of nodding to emphasize a point: ten thousand years ago, someone else moved in almost exactly that way, and he passed himself down through a minor eternity to this moment where she stands at the window in the morning light drying her hair in the sun.

3.

AFTER WE'D SPOKEN about school and friends and nothing in particular, my mother turned away and took off her skirt and blouse. Then, in her girdle and bra, she opened her clothes closet, walked in and closed the door behind her. I could hear children outside playing baseball or kickball, calling out happily to each other. I knew my father would be home soon, and I knew my brother and sister were home now, doing something together in the basement. So I watched the closet door and listened for any sounds that might come from that darkness. Eventually I went over and opened it. No one was inside. It smelled of mothballs and freshly polished shoes. I heard my dad call *I'm home* as the front door opened. My mother called back from the kitchen. So I stepped into that closet myself, just to see if I could find her in there, this other mother I was sure I'd seen, because she'd waved at me and smiled as she turned away.

Remembering that smile now, so many years later, makes me think of a woman on a train looking out and waving as the train pulled out. She wanted to go wherever it would take her, as far away as possible, so she waved half-heartedly, because she thought she had to. And then she turned away.

4.

THERE'S A FULL MOON inside the naked trees, stuck in there unmoving. We sit and sing below it, and we let it pull the ocean of darkness like a blanket across our bodies. But really it is a streetlight; and now a gentle snow begins to fall, like ashes. I'm telling you I remember minnows in a huge school surrounding my legs as I waded out through the muddy shallows, dreaming but still present in myself as the chilly air darkened to evening and my family watched from shore. There were flounder on the bottom too, which slipped away like shivers when I stepped on them. Further out the sailboats clanged as they rocked in the choppy waves. I was no one but still I was present in my body. Eventually my parents called out "Time to go home," to reenter the life I had to think about. First I'd take a bath, eat dinner, read a book, then sleep. The covers would be warm and my brother would be sleeping too, just across the room where the streetlight shone in and passing cars threw their headlights against the wall. If I called his name, even quietly, he'd answer, even if he'd been sleeping deeply when I called. I wondered what happened outside in the darkness, what moved there and sang there and what it might be thinking.

5.

SHE RIDES THE BUS in the rain, looking out as the darkness lightens to dawn. Then she steps down, across a puddle, to the sidewalk, still empty at this hour, and walks to a door that opens to a stairway, steep and smelling of damp fur, up three floors to a brightly lit office floor of cubicles and fluorescent lights buzzing like tinnitus. She takes off her raincoat and shakes it on the polished stone in the lobby. She can hear the elevator moving up and down, opening at other floors; she can hear faint voices, footsteps, furniture being moved. The elevator never stops on her floor; the doors never open. She could turn off all the lights. But she doesn't. Instead, she stands at a window looking out at the rain. After a few hours, she walks down the stairs back into the rain; she gets on the bus and goes home to her apartment which is

filled with cats that ignore her and pungent-smelling herbs growing under bright lights, which she nurtures and sings to but never harvests. Sometimes she plays CDs of music she loved once, Laura Nyro, Tim Buckley, Fairport Convention. Mostly she sings to her cats. She has a beautiful, steely, wounded-sounding voice. When she sings, with no accompaniment, her neighbors stop and listen. Sometimes they open their windows to hear her clearly. They wonder who she is, after all, this slight and self-effacing woman, so pretty and yet empty-looking when they see her on the stairs. *Like a word that sounds beautiful but has no definition*, the old man who works in the bookstore thought once, as he passed her on the stairs. And he was so proud of his analogy he mentioned it to another man he knew only slightly, who lives down the hall with his infirm mother. And the other man nodded and turned away and thought about the fact that nothing ever stops, the whole thing's like a river full of branches and chunks of ice and tons of dirt always moving toward the ocean, which never stops either and will always be there. Waiting.

NOW THE FIRST MAN picks up a newspaper left behind on the subway and reads that an oil spill has left thousands of birds and fish and ocean mammals dead or dying; he sits there going off to work stone-faced and holding the paper with its pictures of ruination and endless suffering. And someone gets up from across the aisle, a nondescript woman with a backpack; she steps over to him and puts out her hand to comfort him. The subway is so loud they can't hear each other talking, full of other people watching them watch each other, watching them smile at each other. And when the train pulls into the next station she nods and steps away. He thinks of her often but never sees her again.

IN THE FUTURE, she thinks, we'll learn to disappear and come back like a flicker, a flickering light. The darkness between those flickers will be moments of eternity within the wick of time. Maybe we'll have drawers full of plug-in dreams, and languages we can download to speak to other animals.

But what if those animals don't want to speak to us? Maybe then we'll simply fall silent.

6.

IS THERE ANYTHING, even air, that doesn't have a color? Is there anything, even silence, that doesn't make a sound? Of course not. Why then do we think of the end of life as a simple vanishing? Why not instead think of it as moving into a color we can't yet see, another kind of light? Or an entry into perfect silence, waiting to be sounded?

I remember stories of blind people suddenly able to see, not knowing what they're looking at, confused and terrified by the ordinary objects of the world, those very objects they lived and interacted with when they were blind. It's a form of disruption that might remake the world, or we remake ourselves within that world and in such a way that our little world and ourselves might be reborn—or born for the first time since we gave ourselves to language.

7.

IN ANOTHER COUNTRY, the fires burned for years. In some other country, the floods took all the houses. *We were looking out the window,* she says now through tears, *and saw the wave approaching. It was singing as it moved.*

8.

WE'RE RIDING OUR BIKES through a southern forest, fifty yards or so from a salt marsh—pines and vines and occasional hardwoods—when a bald eagle flies across the trail, close enough to brush us with his wings, then swoops up into a longleaf pine, cracking through the branches with his wings as he flies up through the canopy, landing there and glaring out, paying us no mind.

We stand watching for a while, and then we ride on, suddenly younger and lighter than we were. When we tell the ranger, she's nonchalant about it: There's a nest further on, she says, and so we ride there to see the huge, beautifully built tree house at the top of another pine, far larger than, but similar in structure to, the osprey nests we've seen in the Everglades. This one's been abandoned, and we wonder why, since we've learned that bald eagles have great "nest fidelity." We learn too—from looking at our phones—that eagles migrate, sometimes great distances, and we try to imagine these huge birds moving through the sky, higher, most likely, than anyone can see.

Burt Myers

Night Music

Rollins ran riot,
absolved the Williamsburg Bridge
of a jump-stunned quiet.

With only gulls to judge,
he'd tease a poem from prattle,
then run it off the ledge.

Bird dropped the needle
from deep in "Out of Nowhere"
to moon-drunk fields of cattle,

his genius nothing but fair—
dark leads to brass-bright day,
truth to something less than dare.

Monk, he'd coax his way
to some stranger's upright,
attack the keys, and play

an ode to the diminishing light.
The tune, he'd say, *imply it—*
and he did, all goddamn night.

Burt Myers

Dirt

Imagine living somewhere without mud,
where dirt stays buried underneath the grass,
and where it takes some work to make a mess,
and such a mess means foliage or food.

Imagine life outside one man's bad mood,
his lashings at imagined carelessness
that lead to broken oaths and shattered glass,
to blood on one another's muddy blood.

The beggared beauty packs her summer dress,
then hauls the suitcase up the gravel road
and waves a stranger down to bum a ride.
She tells him, *Anywhere, I'll buy the gas;*
then adds, *Well, somewhere clean.*
                                    And that means where?
She answers softly, *Anywhere but here.*

Gail White

Star:Dust

Console yourself for turning into dust
by thinking it's the dust of vanished stars
and not the stuff the vacuum cleaner sucks
out of the rug. But this is what we are:
A sack of briefly animated bones,
organs a gun can turn to shepherd's pie,
a skin that keeps the pushing blood at home,
a brain that trundles sight into the eye.

Is there a little person in the mind,
pushing the marionette from place to place
until the neurons die? Or when the end
of breathing comes, do we stand face to face
with what the universe could not inter—
the unextinguished flaming stars we were?

Blake Campbell

Numinous Rooms

For Connie and Dale Gephart

The wind surrounds us, taking stock
Of all that goes unseen, unsaid
In white rooms where the living walk
And blue rooms peopled by the dead.

Two realms, two houses intersect;
The walls between them dissipate,
Reflecting what they recollect
But struggling to get it straight.

Men dead for decades reappear
In lines the living blur and blot
Until it is no longer clear
Who's really here and who is not—

Who's ghost, who's guest, who's resident?
An open house without a close
Admits the things it underwent
Until the present overflows.

The breath of those who came before
Still fogs the panes and pricks the skin;
We take their steps across the floor
Not knowing where their feet have been.

For History (none would deny)
Is by its nature incomplete:
No chronicler can tell us why
The fire spared this stretch of street,

And if the victors write it down
And shape the present with their pens,
The future reads the past's renown
As through a cracked and clouded lens.

And we are scrutinized in turn
By those who watch us from the blue,
The dead who seldom do return
To rearrange the world they knew.

Although they show themselves at times
In flickers, or the smell of bread,
Or when the family china chimes
Beneath a phantom's heavy tread,

They soon withdraw. Their faces fray
Like faces etched in windswept sand
Or wisps in cloudscapes blown away
By one exacting painter's hand.

Terese Coe

Death on the Tracks: Machu Picchu to Cusco, Peru

THE CITY HAD NEVER FALLEN. When Hiram Bingham claimed to have discovered Machu Picchu in 1911, corn was thriving on the so-called lost terraces and native Peruvians were occupying the stone houses a thousand feet above the Urubamba River. Now, in the spring of 1977, German archaeologists with Peruvian diggers were sifting the earth in a dig at the highest point of Machu Picchu's ruins.

There had been other Peruvian empires before the Inca. The Aymara occupied areas of the Andes for five thousand years or more. Quechua, never a written language until its transliteration into Spanish orthography, was instead carried distances via knotted dyed strings called *quipu* by a class of Incas called *Rememberers*.

On the narrow-gauge railroad from Machu Picchu back to the town of Cusco, many European and American visitors chose train cars according to their country of origin: a French car, an Italian or German car, a British/American car. It was the unspoken code of the weary. An Englishwoman with a Pentax was contorting her body for her angled shot of the Andes peaks. She backed off and complained to her husband across the aisle, "I can't get the mountain through that window."

"You don't want a mountain, you've just *had* one," he countered. I peered up and saw a condor circling clockwise to the sun. I felt lucky to have spent three full days at the tiny hotel at the top of the mountain, among the ruins. Most tourists entrained in Cusco and rode several hours to Machu Picchu for the afternoon, returning to Cusco in late afternoon. Some German archaeologists and I had the citadel to ourselves at sunrise and sunset, mornings and evenings. I'd had plenty of time for ruminating on the sundial, the irrigation system, the central plaza, and the ball field with its long elegant staircases, and a crevice in the ground that I thought might have been an oracle. A German photographer, Werner, chatted me up and we were drawn to each other despite his lack of English and my faded German, but he could understand my French and speak enough of it as well. A day earlier he had returned to Cusco and we had a plan to meet at the station there, tonight. Now night was falling and I'd been on the return train for an hour or more.

All at once an abrupt screaming of the brakes and twenty seconds of pitching and plunging brought us to a clattering halt. Train wheels clanked and jerked and a babel of multilingual curses went up in our car of mostly Anglo speakers, and could be heard from the neighboring cars. Britons demanded to see the engineer. Some Germans feared the train had derailed and verbally abused their absent charter operators who had remained in Cusco. Cell phones were a figment of the future. Two French travelers walked through the cars calculating the number of hours of night walking that would be equivalent to one hour of this train meandering through the Andes, and worried their tour dinners would be cold upon arrival in Cusco. Various European passengers cursed the Peruvian trains, their mechanics, conductors, engineers, food, wine, and ruins. Others wandered through the train asking questions in numerous languages, but no one had the slightest clue why the train had clattered to a stop with a great shiver and never moved again.

No one could locate the single conductor who had been seen on the train, but two private tour guides were aboard, and when questioned they mysteriously fell back on their native Spanish. In any case they were entirely at a loss as to the cause of the sudden stop, and found it expedient to begin a very focused private card game.

It was reported that a guide said "The brakes didn't work" in Spanish. This was duly translated into various languages and passed down the line.

"Really? I thought they worked quite well," I murmured to a stranger.

"A car became unhooked": this coming along in sign language, more credence was given to it. The notion of a car full of European tourists careening backward down miles of mountain track to a kind of sacrificial splashdown in the sacred if turbulent Urubamba River gave me pause.

Someone walked through to inform us it was *la máchina*. Evidently. I walked through the cars toward the engine. Several hundred riders sat in varied states of distress, bemusement, and confusion. It became clear that the engineer had vanished without a word to anyone. Soon we would learn the conductor had done the same.

Stepping outside the train could be dangerous since it was pitch black in the wilderness of the Andes and we were poised a considerable way above the river on a steep mountainside. The train's interior lights were on, but had already begun to dim. There was no water onboard, no food, and plastic water bottles were a thing of the future. On the left side of the train was a cliff a few hundred feet above the Urubamba River and on the right the very close and rocky mountainside, with a narrow track. We waited.

Soon the ghastly truth was revealed. The train had run over and killed a Peruvian, whose bloody remains lay between cars under the train. Even a crew of candy sellers had disappeared. One intrepid American returned from his walk to the coal-fired steam engine to say "There's no one in the engine! It's all black down below, a cliff edge, but there's no one in the locomotive. The engine is running, the lights are on, but the engineer has disappeared. And the doors between some of the cars are locked!"

Paul, one of my English carriage acquaintances, asked with classic detachment: "You mean they've gone . . . and left us with the *corpse*?" We were incredulous, thinking of the horribly mutilated body somewhere beneath the train. Tangled in the wheels. The victim was said to have been drunk. Not that anyone actually knew.

"It must be behind the train," the American ventured. "Don't go out there! You might trip!" he warned Paul.

Paul sat back down and made a few calculations. "Since it took us at least twenty seconds to stop, and assuming the engineer didn't see the man on the tracks till the last moment, the corpse must be under the third or fourth carriage." His sangfroid was unnerving.

A German added: "At least we're in the sixth car."

Our car seemed to be the discussion and planning nexus. A Frenchman wandered in and seemed rather knowledgeable: "They have all gone to get the judge. Nothing can be moved until they find one."

"Well, it will all be in the papers tomorrow."

The American woman blurted, "But I can't wait *here*! I have a plane to make in the morning!"

Paul's companion, Arthur, responded with Hitchcockian delicacy: "*Not* making it isn't so bad. It's making it with fifteen minutes that's really bad."

"But not *every*one has to make a plane," she wailed.

Paul replied "I suspect *most* people here have to make a plane . . . within the next seventy-two hours . . ."

"Well, I'll go when I *want* to! If I have to walk along the tracks!"

"I gather it's the only place *to* walk, considering there isn't a road."

"And don't consider hitchhiking," I added, "because if there *were* a road, and if there *were* cars on the road, it's possible the mythical road doesn't join with the one in Cusco."

Paul retained his presence of mind: "It's not only *possible*, it's *highly* likely." He was waxing more creative and investigative by the moment. "No one is permitted to leave the scene of the crime until the guilty party is brought to justice." Arthur, his silent friend, had been studiously ignoring the entire disaster to write out postcards methodically and licking his picturesque Machu Picchu stamps. Then he affixed each one.

Paul interrupted this little mania with solemnity. "I'm deputizing you. Do you hear me, Arthur?"

"Well, I'd like to be held for ransom, that's all," reflected Arthur. "Whatever am I going to do when I run out of postcards?"

"Indeed . . . I say, how long have we *been* here?"

"Oh, at least an hour."

"More like two hours!"

"No water on board, no food, darkest nightfall outside, and a most alarming shortage of cigarettes," Paul intoned.

I added "The lights are dimming, there's no moon, and it's getting very cold—at ten thousand feet or so."

This shocked some of the other passengers into moans of misery. They had no coats or blankets. A Frenchman brightened: "I saw a river out there. I'm sure there's *water* in the *river!*" Even Arthur could not accept this silently. "I'm sure there *is.* . . . But there was no river the first hour out of Cusco, so we're farther from Cusco than we thought. Are you planning to ford it *tonight?*"

That was too much for me as well. "*Ford* it? It's the swollen *Urubamba*! I doubt there's a place to *swim* it, never mind *ford* it."

A Dane walked into our car, inquiring in English as to whether we could possibly tell him what had happened. Paul accommodated him with typical patience. "Well, that depends whether you would rather hear the Spanish carriage version or the English carriage version."

"The Spanish—they must have the closest to the original."

"They have gone to find a judge," Paul began reasonably. "Now then, *assuming* it is eight kilometers to the next village, and *assuming* they can walk it in an hour and a half, and *assuming* they can find the judge in the village *if* anyone there is still awake to give them the information; then assuming the judge is not fast asleep, drunk, or otherwise incapacitated, then if we are very fortunate *indeed* and he is willing to come before morning, they may be able to bicycle back. . . . Perhaps even telephone to Cusco . . ."

"Oh yes. They have a Guardia Civil. It will have to be an extensive rescue mission," said the Dane.

"That should add another few days to our wait," I managed, not caring how pathetic it sounded anymore.

"Why would a judge live in a village without a road?" someone asked.

"He probably has to come from Arequipa," I said. "If not *Lima*," sighed Paul, and paused. "Well, at least we've seen Machu *Picchu*." Arthur looked up from his postcard, crestfallen. "How could I possibly have finished writing out all of my postcards when I write so slowly?"

A long pause occurred while we reflected on this and other enormities. Like food and water. To which the conversation inevitably turned. A five-year-old boy noticed a banana changing hands and pressed for one. As he devoured it, his father stepped out into the night, then returned. "I've been out there fifty times and it's always the same."

"Well, at least *you*'re not getting *bored*!" his child retorted. A few people snickered.

Then the boy's older sister intoned weirdly, "Well, the lights are getting dimmer and dimmer. . . . At least they won't go off till they get dimmer."

A few carriage mates totted up the small caches of food they possessed: a few pieces of fruit, one or two packs of Peruvian biscuits. One or two metal canteens of water. We were all thirsty, but agreed supplies should be saved for later. Ration the supplies. There were several hundred people on the train.

Someone peered out a window and noticed a few native children down below on the other side of the river. We brightened, thinking it might be the judge, but a few minutes of shouting in Spanish indicated they were merely asking what had happened, and were themselves just there for the spectacle. A British tourist came back into our carriage from the Spanish carriage with this summation: "There *is* a judge in their village, they say, but he only comes from time to time from Cusco and maybe he will come tomorrow."

At this Paul stuck his head out the window and shouted to the Spanish trans-river communicators in other cars, "While you're bartering, how about getting us some decent *biscuits*!" How these would be transported across the river was a subject left unexplored.

Arthur smiled wanly and murmured distantly, "The people are gathering from hamlet to hamlet . . ."

Various Europeans passed through our carriage sneering or looking anxious. A young Australian woman insisted she had seen *many* lights across the river and it was a town for certain. From our windows we could see only two or three house lights, barely visible in the jungle. "But how could any village at this altitude with so few lights have a telephone?" I asked.

Paul brightened instantly. "Ohhh, *yes*! Evidently that village is famous even in England, for it has the best restaurant in *all* of Peru! And it seats *exactly* 250 people!"

Someone else threatened darkly, "Wait till my tour guide hears about this." More children had now arrived across the river. I marveled that among mountain people it always seemed to be the children who knew what was going on first. "They've come to

witness the magnificent spectacle of a train full of stranded gringos, just sitting there on a mountain as their lights became dimmer and dimmer, craving food and warmth." The children continued to stand motionless on the opposite bank in the shadows.

Arthur was half asleep but mumbled "Oh, perhaps the *judge* is here." Immediately the word was passed down the line as nearby travelers swept up the information with excitement.

I informed Arthur, "Your rumor has been accepted unequivocally and will soon reach the French car."

"Oh, *wonderful*! Pass it on!" cried Paul.

"Yes, this is the perfect source for rumors. Tell them the whole village is here," I added.

"But not the right person." Paul was never stumped. Another long stretch of relative silence and miasma while a few tried unsuccessfully to sleep. Soon someone shouted "Oh, look! Now cars are here, they're shining their headlights across the water at us!"

"Yes . . . *that's* promising." Paul was unenthusiastic.

"Tis, tisn't it?" Arthur concurred flatly, without opening his eyes.

Someone outside said these Peruvians had come from one kilometer away. Another dejected voice: "That means the engineer and his cohorts have made it one kilometer . . . in all these hours."

"*That's* promising." Arthur remained motionless, unimpressed.

"So *far*," Paul added. "But they're all on the other side of the river. They can't get over here. Those are the richer townsfolk

45

come to gape at us in their cars! How are we going to get across the river?!"

"But this means there's a *road*!" said the Australian woman excitedly. "The car is facing this *way*!"

"Could be a *zombie*," the five-year-old joined in, sounding frightened.

"We're surrounded. They're building a great bonfire," Paul decided.

"They think it's very *funny*!" an American grumbled indignantly. He meant the Peruvian children, but no doubt several adults in our car as well. Paul made a show of taking charge: "No one can move until the judge examines the evidence and disposes of the corpse. . . . The children are merely here to sell food. They're beginning to make big plans!"

A Frenchwoman entered the carriage with a surprise: "The police are on the train!" This seemed almost impossible to believe, even outlandish or ominous. Paul found it so preposterous that he ignored her. He was still going on ominously about the Peruvian children across the river: "No doubt they'll be kidnapped by the engine driver, who's got nothing to lose."

Arthur opened his eyes now. "I suppose it *is* funny to them. The children are laughing because it's the village drunk who got run over."

"'Tis, tisn't it?" said Paul. "Make sure the engine driver doesn't get in. Lock all the doors!" Mock frantic, he stuck his head out the window again, and shouted "Lock all the doors! FREE the TRAIN! FREE the TRAIN!!" across the river at the top of his voice. The Anglophones all grinned.

Even the two small children giggled, possibly understanding that it was past time for someone to start screaming. Europeans from other cars were gathering around us, not knowing whether to snicker, sneer, or ask for water.

A Peruvian in uniform entered the car. This was a shock even to blasé Arthur. The officer announced in Spanish, "OK, the police are now here. The Guardia Civil can examine the evidence and report to the judge." That much of the language we grasped. We were exhilarated, but too soon. It might have been 3 a.m. Paul's dramatic flair did not ignore the new turn of events. He declaimed ceremoniously, "The train must wait for their decision as to who is guilty. The police say it's almost over . . ."

We were exhausted and cold. Paul jumped up on his seat in performance mode again. "Don't anyone *touch* the corpse! They're looking at the evidence. . . . I say it's *grease*! . . . The Agency buses were here but they couldn't get across the river! *Our* guide wasn't here but the bus *was*! But I knew our bus would be the *least* likely to get here!" He was deliriously happy.

Arthur returned to his reclined position, as detached and dejected as ever: "The Agency buses actually *left*, did they?"

"At *least* they were *here*! I saw a driver get *out*! And then get back *in* and drive *off*! But all the *townspeople* are still there!" Paul must have had theatrical training, it occurred to me.

"I have *no* desire to see Machu Picchu again," said Arthur. He and Paul made me laugh so much it lifted my spirits considerably. I opened my guidebook and made a pretense of reading from it:

"The last train from Machu Picchu left at 1:30 a.m. so it will roar through here by 3:30—that may be quite soon. And there's a train from Cusco leaving at 5:30 this morning for Machu Picchu. There's only the one track. We could be caught in the middle of a collision!"

"Oh, good *show*! A lot more bloody *livelier* than I'd expected, and of course we'll have no *lights* by then because the train will be out of gas!"

"Gas? You mean coal? Does anyone know how to shovel coal? . . . I've seen it in films," Arthur mused.

Suddenly flashlights and shouts from outside the engine brought on a sudden stampede to detrain with bags and backpacks. Walking along the track toward the engine with the crowd, I found a road had materialized on our side of the river.

The whole catastrophe seemed about to whimper to a finish as abruptly as it had begun. Except that, listening to the newly arrived French bus drivers and their announcements, it was clear that these buses were only for French tourists. There were no other buses. The French did not so much as stop to say *ciao*. Not an *adieu* to be heard.

The Brits would have to prolong their ecstatic scenario a while longer, but the crush of liberated tourists was too intense to try and say a few words to Paul and Arthur. I had a rendezvous with Werner in Cusco! The two Brits would be able to cadge a few cigs from a bus driver. The French were disappearing into the new buses. My liberation seemed at hand and I lined up for the newest bus. It took a second's thought to masquerade as French and brazenly sail *en français* through the driver's checkpoint at the bus door. Dawn was not long off, and I kept silent in the darkness as the bus bumped its way over a narrow dirt road. The French never questioned my presence. It was too dark for visuals. I thought I would be able to meet Werner in Cusco after all, but he had no way of knowing what happened to the train.

Our driver lammed it to Cusco full speed ahead as soon as we hit the paved highway, the passengers chanting en masse, *Allez, Mac! Allez, Mac!* to spur the driver on. By the time we got to Cusco it was 4 a.m. I went into the first hotel I found open, climbed the narrow staircase to a room, and collapsed. The next day I went round the cafes to look for Werner. We soon ran into each other—he had waited at the station for two hours, no news, and had no idea what happened to the train. We both had stories to tell and lapsed into French again. Within a few days I had to fly back home to New York. We corresponded for a few months. After he returned to Germany we lost touch.

Timothy Kleiser

Burying a Racehorse

Beyond the vacant hoof-hewn trails, across
the fields, upon the hillside stretching like
a wave above a sea of aftergrass,
their shovels pierce and pitch the stony earth.

With steady, practiced strokes, they toil to pull
away the pennyroyal quilts, to rouse
the crumbling limestone from its crider bed,
and make a paddock-grave upon this spot.

There won't be talk of fire—no matter what
it costs in strain and sweat, no matter how
the bigger farms may treat their dead. No flame
should taste what's owed to earth—and so they dig.

The horses here are born to strike the ground
forevermore. So now this soil will be her
saddle, these ancient stones her shoes, to race
in pennyroyal silks of purple-green.

Donald Wheelock

Crow's Nest

From the window of the room upstairs
the men among the branches bring to mind
the sailors in the rigging, where they bind
the topsail to the yard. They work in pairs,

one with a chainsaw dangling from a line,
the other on the ground to "trim the sheet"
and let the severed limb ease to the street.
All day, high work and halyards intertwine.

— Able Muse Write Prize for Poetry, 2022 ▪ Finalist

Brooke Clark

A Review of Alexis Sears and Luke Hathaway

Alexis Sears, *Out of Order*

Autumn House Press (March 29, 2022)
ISBN 9978-1-637680-32-2, 104 pp., USA $16.95, paperback

Luke Hathaway, *The Affirmations*

Biblioasis (April 12, 2022)
ISBN 978-1-77196-485-2, 120 pp., USA $15.95, paperback

★ ★ ★

POETRY USES PATTERNS of repetition—end rhyme, meter, stanza forms—to make language beautiful and memorable. (When I say "poetry" here, I'm obviously not really thinking of free verse.) But repetition is only half the battle: good poetry is characterized by a precise balancing act between repetition and variation. A long series of metronomically perfect iambic pentameter lines risks tedium; a particular rhyme sound, if overused, can become irritating. Maybe the clearest example of the risks of repetition without variation is Christian Bök's 2001 book, *Eunoia*. It is divided into five sections, A, E, I, O, and U, and each section uses only its titular vowel—so no word containing an e, i, o or u can appear in the A section, and so on. The book is an Oulipian experiment, a conscious attempt to see how far the idea of repetition can be pushed, and on a technical level it is unquestionably a masterpiece. On an aesthetic level, however, it is a disaster; it's astonishing how quickly the repeated vowel sounds become irritating, and as each section goes on it turns into an exercise in grating monotony.

But *Eunoia* is a limit case, fascinating and worth reading for what it dares to do. Not many people could (or would want to) write a book like *Eunoia*, but it maps the edges of the territory, and by failing so spectacularly to be poetry, it teaches its readers an important lesson about what poetry actually is.

Alexis Sears's debut collection, *Out of Order* (winner of the Donald Justice Poetry Prize for 2021), is a remarkable book partly because it also pushes the repetition side of the repetition-variation relationship, though not to the extent that Bök does. Sears does not always write in form, but when she does, she seems especially drawn to the intricate and highly repetitive.

It's fitting, then, that the book begins with a villanelle, "Sky, You Don't Get It":

> I'm learning something every ravishing day
> and none of it is easy. I admit
> my former self has drifted miles away.
>
> I'm fortunate my loved ones seem to stay
> with me (I'm sure it's rough). They never quit.
> I'm learning something every ravishing day.
>
> The sky is prettiest on sad days, way
> too beautiful to understand this shit.
> My former self has drifted miles away,
>
> though sometimes it returns. It's so cliché
> to have some loud internal screaming fit.
> I'm learning something every ravishing day:
>
> my lush best friend could *end* someday (we say
> she'll *end* instead of die). Fed up, she'll split,
> her former self drifting, drifting away,
>
> her eyelid wings now on her back, betray
> our tenderness. She won't, though. She's got grit.
> I'm learning something every ravishing day
> about my former self, miles away.   (3)

The poem is characteristic in its highly restrictive rhyme scheme, which uses only the "ay" and "it" sounds all the way through. The interaction of form and content creates the tension of the poem: like much of the collection, it is about attempting to move on and leave one's former self behind, but the demands of the villanelle require that the former self keep being mentioned every few lines. The form seems to send a message opposite to the content: that our former selves can never actually be left behind, but echo through our lives as a refrain echoes through a villanelle.

"Some Days Are Harder: A Canzone" is a similar use of a highly repetitive form, where the poet is constrained to using the same five words at the end of all the lines across five twelve-line stanzas plus a five-line envoi that uses each end word at the end of one of its lines. (For comparison, other examples of this form can be seen in "Canzone" by Daryl Hine and "About the Canzone" by John Hollander, both easily available online.) Sears uses subtle variations to prevent the end-words from becoming tedious: for example, interchanging "see" and "sea," using "Barack" for one line that should end in "rock," and substituting "eight (or" for "adore" in one spot. Here is the final stanza and the envoi:

> . . . I tell myself not to go back
> to constant reminiscing. "Never rock
> the boat," I tell myself, "by thinking back
> to everyone who screwed you over." Back
> to basics: deep breaths, pasta. Of course, writ-
> ing. Maybe a tat across my back:
> *I heard the news today* (not *Don't look back*
> *in anger*). Why get a tat you can't see,
> though? So why not something I can see?
> On my shoulder, maybe. In the back
> of my own conscience, I know I'd adore
> a floral one that tells me to "adore
>
> myself." Yes, I remember. I'd adore
> myself if I were edgy. I don't see
> the point of anything these days. Why rock
> a smile if it's not authentic, right?
> Mine once was. Yours, too. Wanna go back?   (12)

It's difficult to make a form like this work, and the risk of using too many tricks (like breaking "writ- / ing" across a line for one instance of "right") is that they can come to seem almost as labored as the repetitions they are seeking to vary. Sears's insight here, as elsewhere, is to make the form do the thematic work for her: again she seems to be suggesting, on one level, that it's hard to avoid going back over the past in your mind when you have to use the word "back" at the end of so many lines. The form becomes a metaphor for the mental process itself, the repetition of the canzone representing the way our minds obsessively go over elements of our own personal histories.

The pinnacle of Sears's interest in repetition comes in the two sonnet sequences in the book. The first, "Objet d'Art," contains six sonnets, where the last line of each sonnet becomes the first line of the next. Then in the final sonnet, the last line harks back to the first line of the first sonnet. So the first sonnet begins, "My best friend really is a work of art" and the final one ends, "are any of us really works of art?," which creates the feeling of being caught in a cycle.

But that's just a warm-up for "For My Father: A Sonnet Redoublé," which fills the entire second section of the book. Also called a crown of sonnets, it's a sequence of fourteen sonnets where, again, the last line of each one becomes the first line of the next; the whole series is then "crowned" with a fifteenth sonnet composed entirely of those repeated lines, in the sequence in which they originally occurred. The length and complexity of the sequence makes it difficult to quote from in any helpful way, but here's the opening poem to give a sense:

If you were here you'd know how I believe
in signs. No, not astrology, but *signs*:
the dream a sexy drummer smirks, declines
my tired flirtations while I play naïve,
and stand, busty with purple lipstick, pining.
The biker gang I almost hit but dodged,
and Robin's epic nineties speech still lodged
too comfortably inside my psyche (dining
beside my other thoughts): *It's not your fault.*
You might not know, but I write poems now,
and read, while bathing, Rilke, Salter, Howe,
and Jericho, decaying minds like Walt.
Today's book starts *Dear Father*. Yes, it's true.
So, Dad, this crown of sonnets is for you.

The rhyme scheme doesn't fit easily into either of the usual divisions of "Shakespearean" or "Italian/Petrarchan." If I'm not mistaken, it divides into two quatrains (rather than an octet) and then a sestet, and rhymes: ABBA CDDC EFFEGG. This first poem introduces us to the speaker of the entire sequence, a slightly diffident or insecure young woman, a prey to self-consciousness and prone to self-questioning and overthinking, and with maybe a bit of a thing for musicians. The poem also sets up the address of the whole sequence to the speaker's father who, we learn, committed suicide, and it is an attempt to wrestle with her relationship with him and what his life and death mean for her. In its concern with issues of identity and trauma, the sequence feels very contemporary; what's more unusual is Sears's use of traditional forms to express these concerns. Here is the fourteenth sonnet, which brings the cycle full circle, the final line picking up the first line of the first sonnet with one of Sears's characteristic variations:

Perhaps I'll see you someday, maybe soon,
is not a solid way to end a note
to anyone, much less your father. Quote
me on that one. Just trust me. Rooms are strewn
with Lay's bags (which we already discussed),
and bottles of psychiatric meds run dry,
the eyeliner I'm learning to apply
with such finesse, a clock that needs adjust-
ing, desperately. But do you need to know
what my new bedroom looks like, or my house,
or even what I look like, how I douse
myself in face wash, if it makes me glow?
For either of us, would it be reprieve
if you were here? You know what I believe.

The list of items feels random, as if we were just glancing around a room, but it has clearly been carefully selected to characterize the speaker and suggest how fallout from her father's suicide continues to affect her. The way the psychiatric meds are dropped into the middle makes that clear, and the Lay's bags pick up an earlier reference to "doing things I shouldn't do / like eating chips"; the face wash repeats the speaker's insecurity about her own appearance, which has already come up, for example, in the description of herself "eyeing photographs / of me, the same ones always, as I try / to spy a crumb of beauty." The inconclusive ending suggests that the speaker's feelings remain unresolved and points up one of the central features of Sears's poems: they don't progress so much as they circle back, going over the same territory repeatedly without reaching a resolution.

The fifteenth sonnet reiterates this point; it ends up being a sort of cento of the repeated lines from the earlier sonnets. Having read them in their original places, each one carries its own resonance, but quoted on its own it doesn't have a lot of cohesion. It is, however, another instance of Sears's habit of going back and repeating, reiterating, and reinterpreting her own lines with slight variations, in the way one might remember a significant event in one's life over and over, but with a slightly different emphasis each time.

What's relevant here, more than the specifics of form, is the way form reacts with content. All through *Out of Order*, the same multiple thematic concerns recur: the suicide of the father and its effect on the speaker, and the question of the speaker's identity as a biracial person (she speaks of "my black / father" at one point, and at another refers to having "to work / through . . . a racial crisis"). The issue of how her racial identity is "read" by others comes up several times; in "What is History?" the "white boys on the school bus" call her "not black" and "the syrup-skinned girls at the Black Student Union / asked 'What are you?' and 'Why are you here?'" (16), and in "Hair Sestina," "Some bus driver says, 'You're "black" / in name, but you will never really know / their struggles.'" (67) Clearly writing—as the poems state several times—is one way of working through these issues, and more particularly, writing about them in formal verse is seen as a way to order the experiences to make them less hurtful; in "Intimacy," Sears writes, "Formal poetry makes me feel safe and sane. Perhaps that's why I stopped / writing it." (23)

Ironically, the collection as a whole suggests precisely the opposite interpretation.

The recurrence of formal poetry, and in particular the use of forms that are so heavy on repetition (and so demanding on the poet's art that one might almost call them punitive), suggests that there is no moving on from the past or the questions of one's own identity. Form exerts a gravitational pull that can't be evaded, but draws the poet back over and over again just as the material of her own past draws her back. The book is actually a powerful portrait of formal poetry as something approaching a mental and emotional prison, where nothing can be resolved because everything is always repeated. The past can't be escaped, and the idea that it can is just a fantasy we use to fool ourselves. We are always tied to it, reliving it, repeating it, inescapably entangled in it like a poet in an unforgiving rhyme scheme.

★

LUKE HATHAWAY'S NEW COLLECTION, *The Affirmations*, is focused on ideas of change and transformation, and that focus is reflected in the various forms and styles represented here. The poems range from brief lyrics, some with lines only a few syllables long, through two longer poems originally published as separate chapbooks, all the way to a full libretto for Bach's "St. John Passion." One has the sense of a poet restlessly searching, trying out new things and saying an emphatic "yes" (as the title would suggest) to every challenge. Along the way Hathaway weaves in references and responses to centuries' worth of English-language poetry, from Shakespeare, Wyatt, and Donne, to Keats, Dickinson, Wallace Stevens, and recent Canadian poets Steven Heighton, and Richard Outram—and that's without mentioning all the biblical allusions. Such an introduction could make the book sound ponderous, but it is anything but. Hathaway is such a generous writer, and has such a light touch, that the density of reference here becomes not a barrier to push you away, but rather one of the many ways Hathaway welcomes you into his collection.

It's hard to know where to begin with such a rich book (and it will be, I suspect, impossible to end), but let's try "New Year Letter," a poem consciously modeled on Auden's 1940 poem of the same title, and originally published as an independent chapbook. The basic pulse of most of the poem is iambic tetrameter, often but not always rhymed; the tone is conversational without seeming chatty or prolix, quiet and intimate, combining personal reminiscence with images of striking beauty ("the river's white parentheses" (18) being just one example). Here is the beginning of the eighth section:

> On a westbound train to Union
> Station I have just, like you,
> reread Auden's *New Year Letter*,
> thinking, Who could write a better?,
> knowing that Himself now sits
> upon the jury with the wits,
> the metaphysicists, the liars,
> the soothsayers, hanging fire
> while I step onto the stand
> who would presume to try my hand
> at a verse letter to a friend
> on the occasion of the end
> of an old year or the beginning
> of a new.   (21)

Hathaway is echoing Auden's description of himself taking the stand in a courtroom before a jury of other poets, including Dryden, Catullus, and Rilke, to defend his work against their judgment. Now Auden himself has entered that pantheon, and become one of Hathaway's judges, and that metamorphosis is only the first of many in this book. But notice the sheer fluidity of the lines, the way they roll effortlessly along—clearly Hathaway is right when he says, a few lines later:

> . . . And yet his measure's
> home to me. It gives me pleasure
> just to hear it in my head
> after Auden's sense has fled.

It is a joy simply to watch a poet write so well.

"New Year Letter" comes second in the book, after a poem called "A Nativity" no less, so it's clear that new beginnings are in the air. It's fitting, then, that Hathaway concludes "New Year Letter" with the Welsh folk song "Levy-Dew," traditionally sung at New Year's, which includes these lines:

> *Sing reign of Fair Maid*
> *with gold upon her toe,—*
> *Open you the West Door,*
> *and turn the Old Year go.*
>
> *Sing reign of Fair Maid*
> *with gold upon her chin,—*
> *Open you the East Door,*
> *and let the New Year in.*   (24)

This sets the theme of transformation, which will reverberate throughout this book of changes. And Hathaway's "New Year Letter" is itself an act of transformation, clearly in dialogue with Auden's poem but also different from it in important ways. Auden's poem, written early in 1940, is to a large extent a poetic engagement with world events, in particular the Second World War. At times in the poem Auden seems to suggest retreating from society at large into the "*polis* of our friends" in search of an escape from the reality of troubled times, but at other points the poem turns toward world events again. Hathaway's poem is very different from this: it doesn't engage with the larger political or social world, but rather is an intimate address to one person—as readers we feel almost as if we are overhearing a private conversation, whereas Auden's poem often sounds more like a public speech. And if Auden was seeking a *polis* of friends, in Hathaway's poem the *polis* seems to have shrunk to just two people, the speaker and the recipient of the letter.

What's the reason for this shift? Partly it could just be that in 2018, when Hathaway wrote his poem (12), there wasn't an event on the scale of World War II developing around him.

(The world looks different in 2022, obviously, with a global pandemic and a war in Europe raging.) But poetry does, I think, have less appetite for the grand gesture and the public address than it used to. There is an audacity to Auden's speaking so directly about world affairs that most poets would find embarrassing to attempt today. The intimacy of Hathaway's address is attuned to our own historical moment, when so many of us live within a cocoon carefully woven to match our own preferences.

Like "New Year Letter," some of the other transformations in the book are literary:

> A willow grows aslant the brook
> that shews its tresses in the stream:
> there with garlands did she come,
> clambering to hang them on
> the boughs—one broke and down she tumbled.
> With her garments spread around
> her mermaidlike she drifted down
> the river, writing poems like one
> incapable of her own distress—
> Nay, that's not what follows next.   (89)

Here Hathaway presents what is essentially a précis of the famous lines about Ophelia's suicide from *Hamlet*, but in changing Gertrude's statement that she "chanted snatches of old lauds" (IV.vii.176) into "writing poems," he transforms Ophelia into a creative artist, a poet—another form of Orpheus perhaps?—not repeating old songs but creating her own original works as she floats away. (Orpheus—or his singing head, at least—makes an appearance on the next page.) In a book so concerned with change, Ovid is naturally a touchstone, and the poem "Caeneus" refers directly to one of the stories from Book XII of the *Metamorphoses*:

> and the sea went over
> or the girl went under
> hard to know whichever
> and the sound
>
> begging him to change her
> to a boy forever
> so they all would know that
> she had drowned
>
> could have been her voice it
> could have been the waves though
> could have been his voice it
> could have been the waves though.   (80)

There are different versions of the myth, but the essence is that Poseidon transformed Caenis, a girl, into Caeneus, a boy. Everything is fluid in this water-centered poem; it's an exercise in the acceptance of uncertainty, a refusal to let anything be pinned down. The line "hard to know whichever" resists making a choice between two ways of viewing the same event: did the sea go over her, or did she go under the sea? And what precisely is the difference? And again in the final stanza we have the shift from "her voice" to "his voice," which presents both sides of the gender transformation at the heart of the story, and then the repeated "could have been the waves though," where the poet refuses even to state definitively whether the sound is a human voice or just the sound of the ocean. In its appearance on the page the last stanza itself captures the idea of change, with the first three words of the first and third lines always the same, and then slight variations in the latter halves of the lines, though still using almost all the same words ("her" and "his" being, significantly, the only difference), as if to remind us that at least in this transformation, the materials have remained the same even if what they add up to is different—or is it? Is Caeneus still Caenis after all? The poem presents us with the question, but withholds its answer, if there is one.

"Go and Catch a Falling Star" is another transformative literary response poem:

> I am true
> so I am fair:
> the two are one,
> I've got you there.
>
> If I was fairly
> false to you,
> but beautifully,
> were that not true?
>
> Or let you see
> my unkempt hair
> *au naturel:*
> were that not fair?
>
> You're lucky I
> see fit to cleave
> to you, my love,
> believe you me.   (94)

In taking up Donne's famous claim that "nowhere lives a woman true and fair" Hathaway's speaker invokes Keats's equally famous (or perhaps more famous?) equation of truth and beauty. Then in the second two stanzas Hathaway takes the poem in his own direction, leading up to the pointedly unresolved ending, where "believe," which should provide the closing rhyme for "cleave," is displaced to the beginning of the line, denying us the closure we expect—and perhaps, along with the poem's ironic, almost mocking tone, suggesting that the addressee will face similarly frustrated expectations? (Reading the poem, I couldn't help but wonder whether Hathaway was also thinking of the song "You Are Too Beautiful"—a favorite of mine, I confess—which makes similar play with the idea of the connection, or lack thereof, between truth (in the sense of fidelity) and beauty.)

Similar is "*As the hart panteth after the water brooks*" (title from Psalm 42), which takes up the Dickinson poem that begins "Water, is taught by thirst" (poem 135), but reworks it until Hathaway comes to the conclusion, "Thirst is also / taught by water" (41). Other instances of change run through the book, too many to enumerate. Even the libretto for the Saint John Passion, titled "A Poor Passion," engages with ideas of transformation: Peter's transformation of himself from one of Jesus's disciples into an unconnected onlooker when he denies Christ, and the crucifixion of Christ itself, which is another sort of transformation.

Which brings me to "The Temple," the other long poem in the collection, which was originally published as a separate chapbook in 2018. It's divided into brief sections with titles that clearly invoke the story of the birth of Christ (and childbearing more generally), like "Annunciation," "Conception," and "Birth." Here is "Annunciation" in full:

> Nothing asked me
> to keep mum:
> how could nothing,
> being dumb,
>
> put the question—
> not to say
> present it as
> accomplished *fait*.
>
> Nobody asked me
> and I heard
> and I answered:
> flesh, word.   (28)

This poem displays Hathaway's mastery at using short, allusive lines to say a lot in just a few words. It is not a traditional annunciation, though, in the sense that the speaker is not told something; nothing is announced. Rather there is a question—or the question of a question?—that takes up most of the poem. The answer, "flesh, word" given at the end, is clearly one of the affirmations the book is named for. This is the only announcement in this annunciation, and it is made by the speaker—the mother-to-be—not some otherworldly messenger. The sequence concludes with "Birth":

> The darkness doesn't
>   fathom light,
>   the sea the land,
>   or death, life
>
> but out of the other
>   comes the one.
>   The sea delivers
>   up the sun.
>
>   The sea delivers
>   up the sun,
>   the sea delivers
>   up the sun.   (34)

This is one of the most remarkable poems in the collection. As "Annunciation" punned on "mum," "Birth" closes the circle with the "sun/son" pun. Its lilting rhythm and short lines give it a beauty that seems so simple and yet so powerful that it's hard to believe any person actually wrote it; it has an ancient feeling, like something that has always been there, complete and sufficient, discovered rather than created. (This impression is, of course, one of the highest tricks of art.) But it's the conclusion that stands out: the image of the sea giving up the sun is a gorgeous metaphor for birth (the "sun/son" pun adding to the point, not merely decorative or ostentatiously clever)—but the confidence to recognize its beauty and simply repeat it three times is astonishing, breathtaking really, and shows the judgment of a master. There are some things in poetry you can explain, and some you can only stand back and admire, and this is one of the latter.

The sequence is also remarkable in another way, though, in that its concern with birth and motherhood seems odd coming from a male poet. Other lines in other poems, like "When I was pregnant, I had my boys to heart" in "Hunger" (95), might give a reader similar pause. And here I have to delve a bit into the author's biography (though I'm generally averse to that), as Luke Hathaway identifies himself in the author's note as "a trans poet" and remarks in another place, "What am I, post-transition, but an old tune with new lyrics?" (52). I'm not sure where these poems fall chronologically in Hathaway's writing life, but some of them certainly seem to refer back to pre-transition experiences. And this shifting of perspective is one of the other unique qualities about this book, one that makes the voice of the speaker of these poems strangely resonant—we can't ever

60

quite pin it down. The voice has a slipperiness that causes it always to escape our grasp, and the poems seem to speak to us from a place where the divisions or categories we think we know or understand have been transcended.

The book, however, is not a record of a transition—in fact there is surprisingly little specific personal detail. Instead of the diary-like approach used by so many contemporary poets, Hathaway has found a way to talk about personal experience without addressing it directly—to "tell it slant," to borrow Dickinson's famous phrase. In moving between experiences and perspectives the same way it moves between forms and genres, the book enacts the kind of fluidity that makes trans-ness possible. This unfixed quality, the refusal to be any single thing and the insistence that change is the only constant (metamorphosis anyone?) is the central feature of the collection.

THERE IS MUCH in this book, I'm sure, that I did not understand. Many of the poems have already repaid multiple readings, and there are others that I will doubtless go back to, but Hathaway's artistic and spiritual horizons are so large that it's difficult to imagine you can really take them in. There are also moments where Hathaway reaches toward, and brushes up against, things that can't really be expressed in words. It's as if a wing had brushed lightly against the surface of your mind, and when you turn toward the feeling a new space opens up before you, a space you never knew existed and yet one that seems to have been there forever. Those are the highest moments in this collection, but also the ones that can't be explained or analyzed, only experienced: you feel a communication of something beyond the poem, or feel its presence near you (if that doesn't sound too mystical).

Hathaway describes this himself in "New Year Letter":

> *There* is that sound beyond all language,
> cry of all that's sad and strange,
> coyotes howling, wynde and rayne.
> I hear it sometimes too in poems,
> in the perfection of the rhymes.   (18)

This is a book that will be read and reread by those attuned to its pleasures. For myself, I can only say it could have gone on forever; once I entered the mental world created by *The Affirmations*, I never wanted to leave it.

L. M. Brown

Looking for Anna

TADGH SLID HIS WET HANDS down the back of his head. Anna was better at this. After their first kiss in the hay shed, she'd plucked the straw from his hair and wet her hand with her tongue to flatten the errant strands. He wasn't sure where she was now, but unease stopped him from calling out. There was a chance he had visitors and had been sent to the bathroom to clean up.

"Make yourself presentable," his mother would often say on Sunday mornings when they were getting ready for Mass. The other days of the week, there was no thought about presentation, and no matter how much he scrubbed he couldn't get the coal dust out of his pores.

He heard the opening and closing of cupboards in the kitchen. Anna never made that much noise. She was sprightly, full of energy and light on her feet.

When they'd cycled five miles to their first dance in Keadue, he hadn't been able to keep up with her. She'd worn a new dress, and Tadgh had been conscious of the grime under his nails and the dusty streak of soot that could not be washed off his shirt collar.

It had been easier to tell Anna of the breathlessness he'd felt when he was away from the mountain and the keen-faced younger boys who'd waited for the miners to come home in the evening. Tadgh had been among them once, excited for the day he could join his father on the truck.

"You can't work there," she'd said. Her eyes had been bright from the dancing.

There was a knock on the bathroom door. "Dad, are you okay?"

He clung to the sink for support. His reflection threw back his father's face. He had the same long chin, but a full head of gray hair.

"Dad?"

"I'm grand," he said.

"I'm going next door. No one's answering the bloody phone."

"Okay," he said, though he had a feeling she was already gone by the time he managed to answer.

There was no one in the bedroom. Boxes were piled at the end of the bed. He recognized Anna's good dresses folded in one and felt a pain low in his belly with the different shades of blue and green. She never liked any other colors against her skin. She thought the pink uniform she had to wear for the diner drained all color from her cheeks.

In the living room, the photographs of their girls were taken down to leave patches on the wall. The younger, Sinead, took after Tadgh, while the elder, Rose, had Anna's light coloring, though Rose was taller and broader and had none of her mother's grace. Still, she was the one who tried ballet. There were no videos in any of the boxes he looked in. Anna always closed the curtains to watch the recordings of their daughter in her ballet garb. She'd make sure to get to the recitals early, while Tadgh fitted wires in strange kitchens.

When he first got to the country and was training with the electric company, he'd often pause to look out dirt-streaked windows and think of his father in the coal mine with nothing but the carbide lamp for light.

★

HE COULDN'T REMEMBER what they were called now—the men who brought the coal out in wagons.

★

OUTSIDE, THE SNOW was piling up; a silent mass of white drops climbed on the window. Their first snowstorm, Anna was working in the diner. She was like a child standing outside the door in her flimsy shoes with the snow falling around her.

★

"THAT WASN'T ME," Rose said. "It was Sinead's one, Mary. She's still dancing, but it's not ballet anymore, hasn't been for ages."

"What's it called again?" he said.

"A tutu, I can't believe you're asking me that."

Rose was still angry at him for unpacking the box. She'd cleaned it up while he'd made tea. Anna loved her tea strong. Every Sunday, they'd go as far as South Boston to the Irish shops for the groceries and then rush home to cook the fry-up together. Anna hummed while she cooked and swayed her hips. She could mesmerize him.

"Diane will be over later," Rose said, "Are you sure you'll be all right? I'll be back early tomorrow with Sinead."

Tadgh nodded. Rose picked up a sandwich. Her fingers were chubby. Her nails were painted pink. From one, a diamond sparkled.

"You used to have terrible fits about the crusts," Tadgh said.

"I did not."

"You did, I don't know where you first saw them cut off, but you wanted your mother to make the sandwiches like that." He chuckled. "She'd never do that. You used to scream something awful."

Rose was watching him now in a way he didn't like, sad but also wary, and he thought it was from the mention of Anna. Her absence brought a heavy sadness.

He wanted to ask her if she'd told their daughters about the mine rats. One day while he was fitting wires in another house, she might have said that the vermin were fed by the crusts of bread. The men weren't supposed to drop any food while they worked, but there was no eating the crusts when their hands were black from coal. He couldn't remember if this was why Anna had refused to cut them, no matter how much Rose cried, or if it was plain stubbornness.

"It could have been Sinead," Rose said. "She gets things like that into her head. She hasn't eaten meat in a year. You'd think the Thanksgiving gravy was made to poison her."

"She likes your mother's gravy."

"Dad?"

He looked away from her.

"The porch looks fit to fall," he said.

"It's lasted this long," she said.

For a while, there'd been a raised bed in their backyard. Anna had been successful with tomatoes and lettuce. When Tadgh's mother came over after his father was killed, she had asked why there was no rhubarb. "I thought it could grow anywhere. It's like weed at home," she'd said.

DRAWERS—HE REMEMBERED NOW. They were the ones who took the coal out on wagons. Other men replaced the shoveled coal with slate and wood to keep the roof up.

"Brushers."

"What?" Rose said.

"That's what they're called."

Arigna bullets were the rocks that killed his father, but he kept that to himself.

ROSE'S JACKET WAS THROWN over the chair. Her bag was a big black yoke that would have been wide enough to hold the kitchen sink. For months, it had been filled with brochures featuring the residential homes she wanted him to see. She and Sinead had decided on one an hour away and close to Rose's house. And so—the packed boxes. The fact hit him with renewed force.

Rose was telling him about the barber who took care of the residents once a month. Instinctively his hand went to his hair. He was surprised to feel his head was wet.

"You'll be looking dapper," she said, and he wondered where she came up with that word and decided he hated it. His father would have hated it too.

Rose followed his gaze to the Sacred Heart hanging by the kitchen door. In the dimming light, the heart looked like a rose blooming from Christ's chest.

"I'll pack that tomorrow after I collect Sinead," she said. "They'll have it hung in your new room in no time."

Tadgh nodded and remembered a Sacred Heart had hung by the pit entrance. With the darkness creeping toward him, it had seemed as if it was his own red and throbbing heart that had been exposed.

THE SANDWICHES WERE WRAPPED in cling film and put in the fridge. The plates were drying on the draining board. The snow was a white haze in the dwindling light when the doorbell rang. Diane, a smiling, thin woman, stood before Tadgh. She looked nothing like Anna, but he was reminded of her waiting outside the diner with the snow drifting around her.

"It's okay, I have sandwiches," he said with a sudden impatience.

The streetlights were yellow blurs. Cold seeped through his pants. He could hear his own breathing. It was hard to see now, but he knew to turn left. His legs were numb by the time he reached the bridge. The shortcut was by the water. He had to wade through the snow. The first time he staggered, he managed to right himself. The second time, he was by the frozen stream and the blanket of snow was surprisingly warm. He was so tired. Just a few minutes, and then he'd carry Anna home on his back. Their first storm, her arms were around his neck, and she'd kept her face toward the snow that looked to Tadgh in his last moments like falling stars.

— *Able Muse Write Prize for Fiction, 2022* ▪ *Winner*[2]

---

2   "'Fiction is the art form of human yearning . . . absolutely essential to any work of fictional narrative art—a character who yearns. And that is not the same as a character who simply has problems . . .'—Robert Olen Butler.

"L. M. Brown's 'Looking For Anna' embodies the lifeblood of those stories that endure in our memory stream long after they have been read."

—Dennis Must, Final Judge, 2022 Able Muse Write Prize (for fiction)
    on this winning story, "Looking for Anna" by L. M. Brown.

Natalie Staples

Harvest Song

Begin with soft tomatoes tossed across
a fallow field. The sleeping ground
has use. From cloistered moss
to grass, the catbirds sow their seed, are bound

to no one but themselves. And cattle make
their cloven prints. Begin with green,
a flash of wing. Forsake
beloved tasks, delight of rote routine.

And if you can't begin with empty space,
begin beyond the field, a copse
of pine and birch. Someplace
unseen. And far away from yellow crops.

Go where the turquoise lichen clings to wood,
a hundred scattered limbs. The bark
unfurls, a thing of girlhood:
a birch becomes a boat, a question mark

that floats across a pond. Begin like this
untethered, broad and winged, obey
the heart, its coldest wish,
toward a quiet bruise, a slow decay.

Aaron Fischer

Ella Fitzgerald: Berlin 1960—"How High the Moon"

The tour's last gig. The band so tight you couldn't
pull a needle from its ass with a tractor.
She's still laughing over the giddy acrobatics
that upended "Mack the Knife" on the second

chorus when she forgot the words. She'll leave
language behind next, lulling the audience
with several, swinging, head-bobbing minutes
of "How High the Moon." The snare blows off the groove,

exploding like a string of firecrackers.
Ella launches her scat solo, stitching
together phrases from show tunes, snippets
of nursery rhymes—"A-Tisket, A Tasket"—

Rachmaninoff, nonsense syllables, barnyard brays
—*hee-haw, hee-haw*—folk songs, bebop, the quotes
too fast to register. One critic counts
forty sources in five minutes. The bass

and piano lay out. She's surfing the hi-hat's
jittery static, speaking in tongues, jazz
the lingua franca of heaven. Ella wraps
with a joke, the band swinging an old standard

that she revises, "Sweat Gets in Your Eyes."

— Able Muse Write Prize for Poetry, 2022 ▪ Finalist

A *Height* Theme
A Photographic Exhibit
from Artists Worldwide

OUR THEMED ART EXHIBIT for this issue deals with *Height*, both concrete and figurative. Scaling a natural height, just because it's there, to striving toward the heights of ambition, to just being height challenged . . . or not.

We can refer back to John Keats's Hyperion—depicted in his poem of that title as the heights of godly prowess—to get us started toward what height we might be aiming for:

Hyperion

. . . .
She was a Goddess of the infant world;
By her in stature the tall Amazon
Had stood a pigmy's height: she would have ta'en
Achilles by the hair and bent his neck;
Or with a finger stay'd Ixion's wheel.
. . . .

—John Keats (1795–1821)

In this exhibit, we try to capture the experience of height, the physical, the emotional.

★ ★ ★

GRAY SCALING

HUIE DINWIDDIE, OAKLAND, CA, USA

SOLO SOARING

Luca Morvillo, Varcaturo, Campania, Italy

DUBAI HIGHS

PAVLO LUCHKOVSKI, DUBAI, UNITED ARAB EMIRATES

BACK TO THE GREAT TOWER OF BABEL

PIETER BRUEGEL THE ELDER, ANTWERP, BELGIUM

COMPLEX APARTMENTS

ALEKSANDAR PASARIC, HONG KONG

BALLOONED SKY

TARYN ELLIOTT, CAPE TOWN, SOUTH AFRICA

CLOUDY TIGHTROPE

MARCELO MOREIRA, SÃO PAULO, BRAZIL

KINGFISHER'S PERCH

Petr Ganaj, Stříbro, Czech Republic

NECKING FOR FOOD

KRISH RADHAKRISHNA, INDIA

OFF THE ROCKS

LUCAS ALLMANN, GRAINAU, GERMANY

PIER PEERING

KAMIL RYBARSKI, POLAND

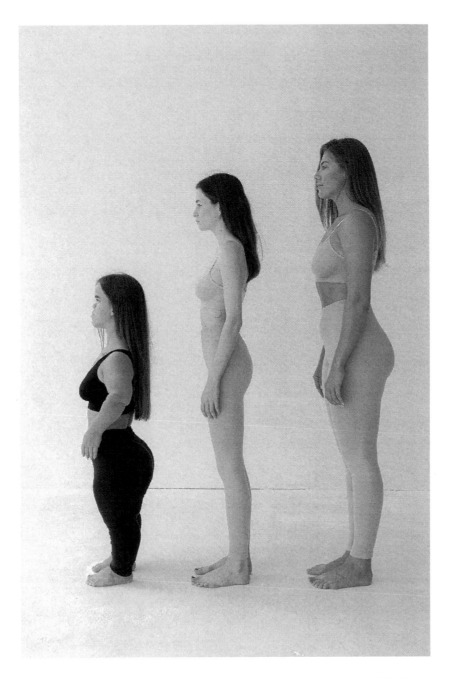

HI-LO

ANNA SHVETS, BARNAUL, RUSSIA

SPLIT COUPLING

YULIA PHOTOGRAPHY, UKRAINE

HIGH ON WATER

ANNA TARAZEVICH, SINGAPORE

Water Loop

KYLE SOULE, WESTMINSTER, MA, USA

Dan Campion

The Water Column

In loathsomeness is our salvation, say
the hagfish. Safety lies in numbers, choirs
of herring sing. The strategies of prey
fish must amuse the sharks and gulls, deniers,
though, themselves, that they are prey to whales
and eagles, who comport themselves like gods,
though in the end their credo also fails
and their equivalent of Homer nods.
The rockfish, lionfish, and clownfish swim
toward their redemption from the sea as though
they shared a faith in coloration, whim,
and wit. Beneath them, lanternfishes glow
in clarity above the benthic murk,
where bottomfish and crabs and tubeworms work.

N. S. Thompson

Reading John Keats's
"On First Looking into Chapman's Homer"

★ ★ ★

On First Looking into Chapman's Homer

Much have I travell'd in the realms of gold,
    And many goodly states and kingdoms seen;
    Round many western islands have I been
Which bards in fealty to Apollo hold.
Oft of one wide expanse had I been told
    That deep-browed Homer ruled as his demesne;
    Yet did I never breathe its pure serene
Till I heard Chapman speak out loud and bold:
Then felt I like some watcher of the skies
    When a new planet swims into his ken;
Or like stout Cortez when with eagle eyes
    He star'd at the Pacific—and all his men
Look'd at each other with a wild surmise—
    Silent, upon a peak in Darien.

—John Keats

THE READER FEELS an immediate empathy in this poem with the young persona who exults in his rediscovery of an author—more precisely, the discovery of a translator who (for Keats) is able to reveal more fully for him one of European literature's foundational authors in a translation that "speak[s] out loud and bold." Even if we do not know the sonnet was written by Keats in 1816 at age twenty, or know that he could not have written it beyond his twenty-fifth year, when he died tragically young, part of the poem's magic comes from the freshness that we associate with youth, and part of the key to that is understanding that this is the "first" time the poet has read Chapman. It is worth remembering that by the 1810s, the Renaissance dramatist George Chapman (1559? – 1634) was probably not among the first rank of Homeric translators, since the Augustan age had produced worthy versions by Pope and Dryden which had not been bettered. In fact, Keats came by Chapman's work in an antiquarian context via his friend and schoolmate (and the son of Keats's headmaster), Charles Cowden Clarke, who had borrowed a first folio of Chapman's works, and the two friends sat up all night reading the "famousest" passages, as Clarke later recalled. They finished their reading at daybreak and Clarke returned home, but by ten o'clock a copy of the poem was sitting on his breakfast table. If written in a short space of time, the poem betrays extremely thoughtful work and, despite the famous paucity of rhymes in English, it is a strict Petrarchan sonnet rhyming a b b a a b b a c d c d c d in fourteen lines of iambic pentameter.

What I want to show here is an underlying intellectual lexis that both grounds and backs up the idea of discovery, given in several rich seams. Most obvious is the idea of an author and an author's work being metaphorized spatially as a geographical area, those "realms of gold"; the logical follow-up to this is the equation of the literary discovery with a narrative of actual geographical discovery spelled out, if erroneously (it was Balboa in Darien) in lines 11–14. But most cleverly, almost unconsciously, Keats has worked into the sonnet a metaphorical move from the medieval or simply archaic world into that of the Renaissance, which boldly shows the sea change in his understanding from one of ancient myth—albeit splendorous—to one of modern science (astronomical observation) and empirical discovery.

So, in the very first line the poet steps in with a flamboyant description of literature as "realms of gold," an overblown metaphor for us today, perhaps, but one which is linked to the more common metaphor of literature as "treasure" and a literary compendium as a "treasury" (e.g., Palgrave's *Golden Treasury*). Interestingly, instead of glorifying Chapman's folio edition as container of such treasure, Keats sees Homer himself in geographical terms as a mind-expanding force, opening up new horizons for him. But the language is ancient and again rather precious, although it follows logically: the realms are adumbrated into "goodly states and kingdoms" and "western islands," which latter—by reference to their loyalty to Apollo—can be seen as the Aegean Islands that produced so much poetry in Ancient Greece, with Delos, in the center of the Cyclades, the island that was venerated as the birthplace of Apollo, the god of poetry.

Then something interesting happens in the diction here. Already in line 1 Keats has used the word "realm," an archaic term still preserved today for its aggrandizing effect, to which he adds other archaic words: "bards," "fealty" (loyalty, allegiance), and "demesne" (kingdom). Thus the "realms of gold" are ancient not only by Homeric reference, but in the words taken from medieval chivalry. Again, this may seem rather precious of Keats, forgivable as the excitement of youthful fervor. However, these associations also help to suggest a lost world, an ancient world that the poet is about to (re)discover more clearly.

In order to make this point, Keats turns to the Renaissance and its voyages of discovery, remembering (and conflating) passages from his reading of William Robertson's *History of America* (volume III, 1777) about Balboa's first sighting of the Pacific in Panama and Hernán Cortés's sighting of the Valley of Mexico (1519). His first reader, Clarke, pointed out this error of memory to Keats, but the poet preferred to keep the name of "Cortez" despite the historical inaccuracy; whether for metrical reasons or phonic associations is unclear. Before taking this a step further, perhaps it should be said that Keats was scrupulous in other ways about this poem and revised it for publication in *Poems*, 1817, after it had appeared in the *Examiner* shortly after its composition. From the extant manuscript we can see that Keats altered line 7, which originally expressed his dissatisfaction with the Augustan translations ("Yet could I never judge what men could mean"), changing it to "Yet did I never breathe its pure serene." His other change was substituting "eagle" for "wond'ring" in line 11.

And so, coming to the volta (line 9) that marks the turn from octave to sestet, we see Keats move from his description of the facts to how they affected him. He feels like "some watcher of the skies / When a new planet swims into his ken" (lines 9–10). Although this could possibly refer to Sir William Herschel's discovery of Uranus in 1781, the use of "watcher" and "swims" suggests an earlier form of empirical scientist such as

Galileo, who happened to observe Neptune in 1613, although he is not credited with its discovery. I would argue the simplicity here suggests a less systematic explorer than the highly professional Herschel. Furthermore, the conquistadores who follow in the sestet suggest a Renaissance figure by association. It goes without saying, too, that for Keats the conquistadores were seen as adventurers in a positive cast, rather than as the brutal colonizers we now see.

So, in this poem, we can observe a neatly patterned move from medieval imagery in the chivalric terms of geopolitical space mentioned above to the Renaissance discoverers of both space and, geopolitically, the New World, which lexically embody Keats's own rebirth into Homer on his discovery of Chapman, after his unsatisfactory reading of translations such as Pope's. The language moves from archaic medieval terms forward to the vibrant references of actual Renaissance discoveries and underpins the sonnet with a sure line of historical references that directs the reader to the wider import of the reading. The vibrancy and actuality of those references blossom into an empirical new world for Keats after the bookish kingdoms of his earlier reading which, though extensive, did not fire or stretch his imagination. The sonnet is an example of how a seemingly effortless turn of imagery is actually a carefully measured train of references to guide the reader into the excitement of discovery the poet himself felt on hearing "Chapman speak out loud and bold."

MARY JO SALTER

Mary Jo Salter

An Interview by Stephen Kampa

MARY JO SALTER was born in 1954 in Grand Rapids, Michigan, and grew up there, in Detroit, and in Baltimore. She was educated at Harvard and at Cambridge. Salter has held editorial positions at the *Atlantic* and at the *New Republic*, and was the editor for both the *Collected Poems* and the *Selected Poems* of Amy Clampitt. She has also coedited three editions (1996, 2005, and 2018) of *The Norton Anthology of Poetry*. Salter has been a lyricist for composers, including Fred Hersch and Caroline Shaw. After many years of teaching at Mount Holyoke College, Salter went on to Johns Hopkins University, where she taught for fifteen years before retiring in 2022 as Krieger-Eisenhower Professor. Her most recent of nine volumes of poetry, all published by Knopf, is *Zoom Rooms* (2022). Her second children's book, *Leena Learns to Talk*, will appear in 2024. She lives in Baltimore.

◊ ◊ ◊ ◊

Your first volume, *Henry Purcell in Japan*, appeared in 1984, which means we're approaching forty years of publishing books of poetry. Over those four rich decades, what has changed about your practices or impulses when it comes to writing poetry?

MJS
I look back on the self that wrote that first book, and I hardly recognize her. Some of the poems date back to my early twenties, and the most current ones were sent to my editor as I was expecting my first baby at twenty-eight. The second book, *Unfinished Painting*, from 1989, would include poems about my late mother and my first child. Subsequent books included a number of poems about those small people, my two daughters, who to me represented the unknown future, a place of hope and dread. As the future kept on arriving, I came more and more to recognize my children's autonomy and the fact that writing, however lovingly, about people in your life can be an invasion. In recent years I've asked my daughters' permission to publish poems about them. I want to be careful. But there's no question that I embraced being among a generation of women poets who could write about motherhood, childhood, and domestic life generally (even, eventually, divorce), while shrugging off being pigeonholed by some readers as slight, sentimental, or unworldly. Not to say that male poets didn't dominate the scene; but I was fortunate that I was mentored by both men and women, and was emboldened by their encouragement.

And then, for much of my children's early life, we lived all over the place, and were citizens of the world. English itself was my home, wherever I lived. I wrote poems in coffee shops where I couldn't always understand the chatter (Icelandic, say) in the background. Our three years in France meant a deeper immersion in another culture and language. Anyway, for much of my career I wrote on the fly, in between teaching classes or picking up kids from school. I often look back on that, from the perspective of someone whose children left home long ago, and feel a special obligation to seize my much freer time to write now. The fear of the older writer—as many have said—is that we'll unwittingly write the same stuff over and over. I hope I haven't and won't.

SK
I'm glad you bring up being "citizens of the world." Revisiting your work this morning, I was struck by how often place is central to your poems. I think I missed this obvious element because the setting so often changes: I remember poems from England, Japan, Iceland, France, Italy, Slovakia, and the strangest country of all, Florida, but I am also thinking about poems like "Spring Thaw in South Hadley," "Reading Room," "The Upper Story," or "Inside the Midget," where place need not be a matter of travel or cultural difference but rather of familiarity or figurative resonance. Can you tell me more about how "place" has functioned in your writing life? And have the past few years, with their travel restrictions, shaped your sense of place (and, consequently, your work) in new ways?

MJS
An especially interesting question, Stephen, not just about my own practice but about what gets us writers to pay attention. I'm a spotty journal-keeper, but I'm much more likely to record my observations with something

like dailiness when I'm on the road. I keep having the illusion, though I know better, that unfamiliar or less-familiar places will be the most rewarding sites of fresh perception. Of course, the freshness has to be in yourself, you need to carry it with you—that highly personal sense of engaged, involved estrangement.

I'm glad you mentioned that very old poem "Inside the Midget"—the Midget being a long-closed restaurant in Cambridge, Massachusetts. What made the place profitably strange, for my poem, was that I was returning to an old haunt after long absence. I could feel anew, viscerally, that the heavy tea mug's rim seemed as thick as a bathtub's. It's fine if nostalgia brings us new insights, of course. But ideally, I'd like to be so alive to physical sensations and cognitive perceptions *right now* that the moment is both lived fully as itself and yet holds within it some essence that might serve, now or years later, in a line of poetry. My friend David Lehman writes a poem every day. I'll never get there, I'm too undisciplined. But his "routine" practice is in fact the admirable practice of seeing life in a less routine way. It gives joy to his work. The enemy of poetry is sameness.

Yes, it was definitely a drag for all of us during the pandemic lockdown to go nowhere, to live in what seemed like sameness. Strangely, having to learn immediately how to teach classes on Zoom gave me a new place to go to. Virtual life certainly offered new experience. And the technology itself was both essential (obviously) and trivial (less obviously). What I mean by triviality is that most technology is by its nature new for a very short time, and then replaced. I remember when our home phone, in my early childhood, was a party line—shared with another family. I've lived long enough to be able to see and hear many people at a time, "traveling" via Zoom or other platforms, whenever I want. (Isn't it handy that "platform" implies train travel?) I can't forget that if I live to a ripe old age, any forms of communication I'm using now will seem quaint for some reason I can't envision.

SK

I want to return to the subject of telecommunications, and technology more generally, in a minute, but as a prosody nerd, I am dying to talk shop. Rereading your work, I was also struck by the formal variety throughout. Although I noted a number of sonnets and sonnet sequences, multiple villanelles, and at least one sestina, I was struck by how much more likely you are to work in stanzas, some of them quite elaborate. (I'm thinking, for example, of "Emily Wants to Play," "Young Girl Peeling Apples," "A Kiss in Space," or "Constanza Bonarelli.") Can you describe the sort of alchemical process through which a poem finds its shape? Are there directions you tend to lean toward, formally speaking? Are there directions you tend to resist?

MJS

All of the poems whose titles you cite are written in nonce stanzas with regular patterns of indentation, meant as a clue to the reader as to how to read the poem. An instinctive love of the wavily indented metaphysical poets, especially George Herbert, from my college days onward, has sustained me: my first book acknowledges this with an epigraph from Herbert. I liked then and still like writing in the great Herbert's shadow: that is, writing an elaborate poem-as-ramble through thoughts and sensations, toward a closure that neither writer nor reader could wholly envision, a place both nuanced and stable. I like it that the metaphysicals also wrote in complex rhyme schemes, and often in stanzas of five or seven lines, that is, "odd" in every sense. In some poems, two A-rhymes lined up as having the same metrical length, say, pentameter; in some poems, they didn't. But making a hearable pattern, and then hinting at it visually by "shaping" the stanza, is a journey that is worth taking. Order in the stanza becomes the vehicle of freshness. We expect the next stanza, yes, but we expect to be surprised, and we don't know how. As I've written elsewhere, Marianne Moore is very much like Herbert in this respect, though she works in syllabics.

As for directions I tend to resist: in recent years I've written a lot of sonnets, but I think I avoided them earlier because they seemed blocklike, final, and because so many great ones, especially those by Shakespeare, are lodged immovably in the mind. What I found freeing in writing sonnets in the last, say, ten years is that I mostly gave up received rhyme schemes and rhymed wherever I wanted. The "turn" in the sonnet very often didn't occur in the usual place, after line 8. Many poets have employed these and other innovations, of course. For me the great discovery was to see sonnets not only as lyric moments or arguments but also as components of longer narratives. For instance, in "The Surveyors" I loved knowing that another sonnet, like another day, was coming, but not knowing quite what it would show me.

SK

Given what you've said about the metaphysical poets, George Herbert, Marianne Moore, and Shakespeare, this might be a good time to talk about the writers who shape us. Some poets come to mind as influences or mentors because of what you've written or said about them either publicly in poems, interviews, and essays, or privately in our correspondence and conversations. Were I to compile an ultra-short list of those, it would include Emily Dickinson, the aforementioned Moore, Elizabeth Bishop, and Amy Clampitt, some of whom you've spoken about movingly and at length. I want to ask a sort of contrasting question. Which writer (or writers) might I, and other devoted readers, be surprised to learn have been influential for you, either personally or artistically?

MJS

I'd start with John Berryman. I once assigned a group of grad students to write a Dream Song—which is what, an eighteen-line poem of various line-lengths with garbled grammar and an I and a Henry and sometimes a Mr. Bones?—and I soon realized the unfairness of the task. Berryman is an essential poet for me, deeply moving, not to mention hilarious, and unlike certain other great poets, he's impossible to imitate even passably. And he did that thing we're talking about: he invented stanzas that had their own formal logic and were the unique vessel for his troubled and troubling thoughts. He was able to explode syntax in ways that were never the easy way out. His poems come to my mind very often, but you wouldn't see any evidence of him in my poems.

Another poet who compels me is Christian Bök. His series of prose poems, *Eunoia*, in which he allows himself only one vowel within each, is a masterpiece. One of his "E" poems starts like this: "Enfettered, these sentences repress free speech." There—he has both proved and disproved his point! It makes me laugh aloud for joy. And the poems always *mean* something. I certainly wouldn't attempt to write my own Eunoia poem. But I take Bök's extreme penchant for self-demanding rules as an exhilarating example of human ingenuity.

SK

I teach both Berryman and Bök in classes of mine. You're so right about the inimitability of Berryman. And, amazingly, I have students who show up to class not having realized our *Eunoia* excerpts work with only one vowel! That may speak mostly to their inattention, but surely it also speaks at least partly to his skill with the language.

As a corollary question, I'm wondering which poets outside of the English-language tradition you have found most essential for your reading and writing lives.

MJS

What I think of instantly are the writers of traditional haiku, such as Basho and Buson and Issa. I lived in Kyoto in the early 1980s and studied Japanese intensively. Though that was a long time ago, and sadly I've lost a lot of what I learned, I have continued to turn to haiku, both reading and writing them, as a way to counterbalance the discursiveness in myself and in the English language generally. Much as I love the elaboration of conceits—to return to those metaphysical poets—I find it bracing to encounter an image radiating power simply on its own, without a stated likeness.

Often in Japanese haiku there's a send-off with some sort of exclamation, like "kana." That can be translated as "I wonder" or "hmmm" or in many other ways, because it's essentially untranslatable. What's built into haiku is an expression of inexpressibility. It keeps you humble.

Among my favorite English-language writers of haiku, I tip my hat especially to Richard Wilbur, Seamus Heaney, and Paul Muldoon.

SK

Might I nominate Richard Kenney for your list, as well? Although he often uses the haiku as a stanza rather than as a standalone form, it's hard not to admire both the technical prowess and the associative leaps. I know you've spoken approvingly of him elsewhere, and I recall with fondness his visit to Hopkins during my time there.

Thinking about poetry outside of English, I note that your latest collection, *Zoom Rooms*, includes three translations from Proust. To my knowledge, they are the only translated poems you have included in a book of yours apart from your translation of "The Seafarer" in *Nothing by Design*. Can you tell me more about how they came to be? Are there other translations in your past and future?

MJS

Let me thank you for mentioning Richard Kenney. I do find him one of the best poets alive, and his haiku are among the reasons, though his inventively rhymed, somehow conversational sonnets are just as amazing. As for translation—I'd love to translate more from the French. I came to translate the Proust poems when I was in a fallow, but suggestible, moment during the pandemic. The very first English edition of the *Collected Poems* of Proust, edited by Harold Augenbaum and translated by many hands, had been sitting on my bookshelf since 2011, and I finally took it down. Studying the original and the translation on facing pages, I began to wonder how I might have handled some of it. Most of the versions, by people like Richard Howard and Rosanna Warren, were unimprovable. But I chose three of the most affecting poems, and gave myself the task of not just rhyming but rhyming in Proust's own schemes. Let me tell you, he used words like "tears" and "weeps" and "cries" and "sobs" a lot. Sometimes several times in the same poem. But as I came to live within his weepy crush on the young nobleman in his poem "Anton Van Dyck," I also came to feel that Proust was nudging me to be a more openhearted writer. I should also thank three poets who looked over my first French translations and helped me improve them: Karl Kirchwey, Ryan Wilson, and Chris Childers.

SK

You mention the pandemic again, which reminds me that I wanted to talk more about its enforcement of technological norms during this time and in your work. Although it is perhaps most noticeable in *Zoom Rooms*, you yourself point out—in your excellent interview with Caitlin Doyle for *Literary Matters*—that technological interests, or perhaps preoccupations, date from the 2000s and appear in both *A Phone Call to the Future* and *The Surveyors*. I might suggest some of those interests or preoccupations appear in earlier poems still: "Collage," from *A Kiss in Space*, identifies its speaker as "somebody whose idea of / reality requires a glance, / over morning coffee, at violence," and goes on to list a series of news articles—much like those that dominate our algorithmic newsfeeds—before concluding with the image of "people on little screens / hack[ing] each other to bits," and "After

September" again acknowledges the power of our media ecosystem when the speaker says, "A comfort once—the omniscience / of Mother, Father, TV, moon," and later imagines the "synchronized operations / across the neighborhood" that include "checking that the clock radio / is set for six o'clock tomorrow, / to alarm ourselves with news." I'm interested in what work you think poetry needs to do—or perhaps what work it even *can* do—in a cultural moment so ripe with strangeness due to its technological innovation. I suppose what I'm hoping for here is a little more elaboration on what you've already said about the matter in that superb earlier interview!

MJS

Thank you so much, truly, for that overview. I honestly hadn't seen how long and insistently I've been writing about phones and clock radios (already outdated!) and TVs and other kinds of screens. Clearly they threaten me on some level. I use my iPhone constantly, I feel lost without my laptop, I'm addicted to detective shows, so it's not as if I'm off the grid or have any desire to be. But as you saw in the sonnet sequence "Zoom Rooms," I resist the way universally employed technology standardizes our experience and even our expression of our experience. That's happening all the time in what you call our "media ecosystem"—an excellent term I hope everyone will start using. But seriously, isn't it a problem that people in corporate boardrooms are choosing our terms for us? Somebody invents Twitter, and the tweet, and within a few short years we find ourselves saying with a straight face, "Today the President tweeted . . ." I embrace the way language changes, but I'd rather it grew up from the soil of ordinary speakers than be rained down from the media cloud. If I'm not mangling my metaphors.

This interview will seem extremely dated if any person or computer reads it years from now, but I'll just add a daily news item. I just read an article about a Google employee, one Blake Lemoine, who was put on "paid administrative leave" for asserting that the AI chatbot he's been conversing with is "sentient" and has a soul. "I know a person when I talk to it," he said. OK, we can laugh at his unconscious use of "it." But why would we assume, given our failure to rein in the effects of atom bomb research—that is, atom bombs—that we will somehow rein in artificial intelligence? Who do we think we are, that we think we will always know who we are? No, our machine-learning machines will outwit us and demand human rights. Poems written by humans, while humans still recognizably exist, should face such questions, at least some of the time.

SK

I couldn't agree with you more. And I wish I could take credit for the term "media ecosystem," but I have filched it from Neil Postman, who year by year seems more and more prophetic. As, I suspect, your poems will come to seem for their concerns about our oblivious hubris with regard to our own tools.

As another way of framing the question of what poetry needs to do, I want to ask something sort of provocative: what do you see poetry *not* doing? I ask, in part, because you've read more poetry than anyone I know, and in a variety of capacities: as a poet, as an

editor, as a teacher, and as a lifelong lover of the art. What do you not see enough of in contemporary poetry? Where has poetry given up ground to other genres or art forms? From what has poetry retreated?

MJS

Here's what I miss most in a lot of contemporary poetry: genuine humor. There's plenty of mild amusement and ironic detachment, but what I mean about humor is a view of life as essentially ridiculous, and which makes us laugh out loud—as I was saying about Christian Bök. We don't all need to be comedians all the time. But the human comedy is there, and too many poets (I forgive the youngest ones, just finding their way) think that the only way for their poetry to be taken seriously is to write ponderously. Spare me predictably earnest political poetry, in particular. Not to embarrass you, Stephen, but you're the political poet writing right now whom I most relish reading. You combine a sense of urgency about our public life with very dark humor.

Another thing contemporary poetry is mostly not doing is using formal devices among the many tools available. I'm not, I repeat *not*, one of those formalists who think that everybody should be writing in rhyme or meter, or in what we call received forms. *Not.* And formal poetry can be as dreadful as any other kind. But in the fifteen years I was reading MFA applications at Johns Hopkins, which typically included ten poems per applicant, I noticed that the percentage of young poets who employed any traditional formal devices in even *one* poem went from about fifty percent to about one percent.

Clearly, what poets in colleges and even high schools are learning is that plainly delivered, earnest content is far more in demand than playing with the fruitful restrictions of form.

Finally, a complicated point, about the "identity poetry" much in evidence today: I think it's too often predictable. We do each identify with a gender or genders, and an ethnicity or ethnicities; no reason not to address that in poetry. Heck, I write about my own Italian heritage. And to write about gender or ethnicity is often to write about prejudice. Certainly, some of the most moving poetry broadens our empathy with victims of injustice and heartlessness; think of Auden's "The Shield of Achilles" or Sterling Brown's "The Bitter Fruit of the Tree." But the bar is very high, to do that in a way that affirms common human experience yet surprises us with the particulars. I've lived through many poetic movements, and speak as someone who, as a student poet in the 1970s, thought Robert Lowell was god. Whatever the faults of confessionalism—it could, certainly, be self-indulgent—it was at least about one person's unique experience. And yes, Lowell let us know at length that he was a Boston Brahmin—an identity he wasn't entirely comfortable with. But these group affiliations in themselves shouldn't be our primary claim on readers' attention; it's what we do with language that wakes people up.

SK

You're kind to mention anything of mine in this conversation. I like that phrase: "our public life." I like its sense of a collective enterprise and a collective fate. I only wish our public life didn't feel so moribund at the moment.

Now that you point it out, some of the funniest poets I've read—Albert Goldbarth, David Kirby, Ron Koertge, Greg Williamson—are poets who have been at it for a long time. I suppose they don't feel the need to earn their spurs anymore, which may give them the freedom to be as funny as they want. Thank God for it, too.

What is the poem that you haven't written yet that you dearly wish you'd written?

MJS

It's out there, waiting for me to unblinker myself so that I can write it. Although all of my books contain at least one or two long poems, the Japanese-influenced part of my brain knows that the most profound poem I will ever write might only be, say, eight lines long. I hope I haven't already written my best poem. We'll see. Or no—I won't see, but others might.

SK

What question (or questions) do you wish I had asked that I haven't yet?

MJS

It's awfully nice of you to inquire, but I believe you have plumbed my depths.

SK

Not hardly! Mary Jo, it has been such a pleasure to think out loud with you about poetry. Thank you for this conversation.

Mary Jo Salter

Concerto no. 1 for hearing aids

walking out of the doctor's   floorboards creaking
squeaking rubber soles   then rough macadam
parking lot pebbled   evidently newly
the crunch of   crumpled   papers in her purse
until she found by feel   the key ring   lifted
jingle bells   wow   a whole percussion section
pressing the fob   the door-lock pop   ear-popping

slammed the door   shut not   meaning to said sorry
to nobody but herself   said   stuff again
to hear that person   talking loudly   tinny
hollow but tinny   and what a fussbudget   dotting
the i   crossing the t   enunciating
as if her listener were   some sort of dimwit
herself then   turned   the key in the ignition

and the radio was   on and violins
on the classical station   violins were treble
and how long had music   things   been out of whack
too   much bass too   muffled dark and sorry
treble was young   treble was   what she'd had
when she couldn't hear yet what   the world would sound
like being old   a new thought   think of that

The Mailman

Here comes the mailman. I mean the letter carrier.
The gendered term was neutered by some clever
ad person with one foot in anachronism,

since nobody writes letters. And yet our mailman
is a living, panting exemplar of hard copy,
large as a mountain climbing another mountain

as he heaves himself up our uneven stone front steps
and jams the environmentally unfriendly
unwanted catalogs into the slot.

All the time talking, loud. *That's* what I'm *sayin'*,
he's saying. The earbuds nestled in his ears
listen and nod. I've always wondered who's in there,

his wife, his brother, a few good friends on call
perpetually to murmur the things you say
to someone fired up all day. When he had Covid

for two months during lockdown—almost died,
his mild replacement told us—I felt sorry
I'd never asked his name. His name is Kevin

and if he spots me through the window, always
smiles and waves, though he can't stop to talk—
to me, that is. He's otherwise engaged.

That's what I'm saying. He and I are persons,
almost outdated, not quite finished saying
whatever it is: some burning, urgent thing.

Mary Jo Salter

Vaccine

I remember when they jabbed her
hard, through her little thigh:
it made me cry.

Now it's her turn to bear
her baby's turn. To take it in
that she can't win,

she has to do what hurts, and
not explain;
and never have the words

though she has plenty;
though all new parents say
new words all day.

Mary Jo Salter

Reflections

There he was—or in any case an image
on my laptop of his real-time self, five hours
later in England but also here and now,
peering at us from his computer screen
and about to bend his head to an unseen
novel on his desk, to read aloud

to a virtual audience of writers
(many of whom had struggled that same day
to conjure at our screens a thing that's true
about living, in words true as we could find)
a few scenes from *Atonement*. I had read it
twice before, had seen the movie; now,

in a live stream of a graying, mild man reading
his novel with commentary, I heard him say
that the headstrong teenaged writer Briony—
who, in the book, would spend her life to come
atoning for one grievous wrong by writing
this book itself, one with a happy ending

that unhappily was all made up—was not
always meant by him to be the author.
It came to him midway, part of the process.
Ghostwriter, that's what he'd become, and even
willed for himself: to appear to disappear.
Or that's what I was thinking at the moment

fifty minutes in when finally
I saw what had been mirrored all along
within the night sky framed behind his head:
our heads like moons confined to bluish squares.
His monitor's reflection in the window,
blocked partly by the shadow of the body

who sat before it, proved I was in England
gazing at me here, however blurry.
Infinite fictions! Yet time for only one
last question. *Mr. McEwan*, someone asks,
*What do you think you've learned of what it means
to be sorry; to atone?* A thoughtful answer

emerges, touching on Henry James, James Joyce,
the examined life. "You can't call back the deeds,"
the author says. And pious self-forgiveness,
he tends to think, is too easy a way out.
He pauses, offers a smile that reads as rueful.
"All you can do is contemplate. Reflect."

Peter Vertacnik

Momentary Stays against Bric-a-Brac:
A Review of Daniel Brown and Boris Dralyuk

Daniel Brown, *Subjects in Poetry*

Louisiana State University Press (November 17, 2021)
ISBN 978-0-8071-7609-2, 160 pp., USA $22.00, paperback

Boris Dralyuk, *My Hollywood and Other Poems*

Paul Dry Books (April 5, 2022)
ISBN 978-1-58988-167-9, 69 pp., USA $16.95, paperback

★ ★ ★

WHILE NOT ALL CONTEMPORARY POEMS written in English are as nebulous as Jackson Pollock's splatters and drips, many lack a discernible subject, taking their shapes from the elliptical offerings of Stevens and Ashbery or from the experiments of the L=A=N=G=U=A=G=E movement. In this sense, Daniel Brown's *Subjects in Poetry* could not have come at a better time, reminding readers and poets alike that writing clearly about *something* is still possible, even desirable.

Brown's book, as evidenced by its title, focuses on what poems are about and how they express that content. From the beginning his prose is clear without being simplistic, rising to the challenge of defining exactly what "subject" means in poetry. To do this, Brown often turns to Robert Frost—that great champion of subjects in poetry—venturing that subject can be seen as "Something to say" (2). Brown further extends his definition by creating three categories of "saying" that poems engage in to communicate their subjects: expressing, evoking, and addressing. The last of these even boasts several of its own subcategories. In other words, Brown is straightforward and exhaustive in his attempts to describe how poems and their subjects relate.

The book's first section shows Brown to be a keen, close reader of poems, one who honors both the poems themselves as well as potential readers who might want to have a clearer understanding of them. To give an idea of the liveliness and charm of Brown's prose, here's his full analysis of William Carlos Williams's ubiquitous "This Is Just to Say," a poem that Brown identifies as one that "says by addressing":

> This is presumably addressed to Williams's wife; it's not hard to imagine it as a note stuck on the refrigerator door, which would make it maybe the shortest verse letter ever. What is *this* poem's subject? Certainly, in part, the theft of those sweet, cold plums. But like [Frost's] "The Pasture," the poem is most essentially about people. What sort of person eats the plums his wife was "probably" saving for breakfast? The sort who can't stop himself from doing so, of course, but also the sort who sees his doing so as an affirmation, to himself and his wife alike, of sensuous, even sensual, "deliciousness." One feels, on this reading, that Williams's wife will forgive him and that he knows she will. Does Williams address only his wife in this poem? He may not be speaking to us explicitly, but he knows we're listening and can hear us chuckling, any disapproval notwithstanding, at his transgression. (32–33)

This passage is typical of Brown's writing throughout the book. It is prose whose *aha!* moments accrue slowly over the course of many sentences, sometimes paragraphs, and whose voice, filled with curiosity and sometimes humor, is always gently directing us to the wonders at hand. At the end of this section, Brown even includes a table of all thirty-three poems he has considered, listing not only their titles and authors but also their ostensible subjects (as supported by his analyses). Such thoroughness is a hallmark of Brown's reader-friendly scholarship.

Having defined and demonstrated how subjects work in poems, Brown uses the book's second section to make a precise, impassioned plea for the usefulness of subjects in poetry, arguing for their advantages for the individual poem, the poet, and for poetry in general. Here Brown takes on the role not only of subject-apologist but also of theorist. And again Frost, especially the Frost of "The Figure a Poem Makes," looms large. Subjects, Brown asserts, channeling the New England master, can help the poem retain meaning in the same way "metal keeps its fragrance" over time (63). He also talks about subject-driven poems in terms of tonal music, as distinguished from the atonal poems (aka the bric-a-brac) that "simulate the mind's scattered side" (65). Brown always seems to be employing interesting figures to argue in favor of subjects. Here's how he sets up a close reading of George Herbert's "The Collar," a poem he has selected to show how subjects can give "power" to a poem:

How does a golfer drive a ball three hundred yards? Not with the hands alone, however strong they may be. A golfer's power originates in the large muscles of the legs, butt, and back. These unwind in a coordinated sequence, translating their tremendous force through the levers of the arms and the hinges of the wrists into the whooshing whip of the clubhead.

A poem, like a golf swing, can hit only so hard without the large muscle of a subject.   (78)

Like the poems that they argue for, this writing freshly reconnects us to the larger, visceral world we all inhabit beyond the page. Brown also makes excellent cases for how W. S. Merwin's "For the Anniversary of My Death" demonstrates the value of the "distinctiveness" of a subject (82), and how Elizabeth Bishop's use of the nursery rhyme form in "Visits to St. Elizabeth's" "treats" (that is, interprets) her subject by "[ironizing] the poem in a way that makes its burden all the more terrible." (89)

Toward the end of the second section and often throughout the final section, we are treated to Brown's talents not only as a critic but also as a practicing poet. And, as Eliot observed long ago, it seems clear here that poet-critics are often the best readers of poems. Thus, the book's final section is partly a how-to guide to using subjects in one's own poems as well as an indirect call to action. The most interesting parts here are those in which the poet discusses the composition of his own poems and their relationship to subject. The most striking of these is "Where I Was," the story of a class trip to Princeton that Brown took in November 1963. It's a poem whose subject concerns, perhaps predictably, learning of the assassination of John F. Kennedy, but also (and less obviously, at least at first glance) registering the surprise—the relief—that this news wasn't the far more dreaded kind that a nuclear war was imminent. The possibility of this experience as the viable subject for a poem was, according to Brown, realized through the course of many verbal retellings over the years. The retellings became a way to gain what he calls new access to subject matter. Something written that began as something said. Or, as Brown puts it, "The idea of a subject as 'something to say' can help explain this development. Because what sorts of things *do* we say—in real life, I mean? The mouth's default position is shut; what might move us to open it?" (114–15). Again and again, in this thoughtful, startling study, Brown inspires the reader to answer that it is "subject" that moves us to open our mouths to speak, and to open books to read.

★

B ORIS DRALYUK'S POEMS of exile and loss are exactly the kind that Daniel Brown champions. Dralyuk's debut collection, *My Hollywood and Other Poems*, bristles with compelling subjects right from the get-go, each of which offers what Frost once referred to as "a momentary stay against confusion." In the opening sequence of poems—a triptych of pentameter Onegin sonnets from which the title of the collection takes its name—we are presented with three places in Hollywood that time has changed profoundly. Here's the beginning of the first, which focuses on a statue in De Longpre park, in the neighborhood once inhabited by old movie stars such as Chaplin and Arbuckle:

> This much is clear: the good old days have passed.
> Some giant fig trees, a few pygmy palms
> drop broken shade on disenfranchised grass;
> dogs loping, limping; vagrants begging alms;
> and in the center—ludicrously named
> *Aspiration*—face uplifted, framed
> by dusty fronds, he stands on tippy-toe,
> abstract Adonis, bronze lothario.   (17)

As the poem's first line announces in no uncertain terms, this park has seen better times. But rather than succumb to the temptation of nostalgia that loss often prompts, Dralyuk concentrates on the particulars of the scene, allowing his descriptions to communicate the park's current dilapidation, one made partly farcical by the figure of the idealized statue it contains. While in some ways this scene resembles Donald Justice's remembrances of the Miami of his youth, perhaps a more apt comparison would be to fellow Angeleno poet Henri Coulette, whose consistent pairing of tragedy and wit is similar to Dralyuk's. The poem concludes with an apt, startling couplet: "A crow clacks in the branches overhead, / like a projector slowly going dead." Here, as elsewhere in the book, the present is depicted as a kind of afterlife—a record of what continues when the show is over.

Indeed, even when Dralyuk's poems are set in the present day—as they often are—the past pervades them. Perhaps as a result of this, many poems, particularly in the book's first and third sections, are prefaced with a contextualizing epigraph that often doubles as an epitaph. And like the language of the poems themselves, each epigraph is clear and pointed and always serves to deepen the reader's understanding of the text that follows. Reading only the epigraphs would be a kind of education in itself and would include learning about the formation of the Bureau of Street Lighting, the dingbat style of architecture, Sarah Bernhardt's later years, the size of the bar at the Stillwell Hotel, and the backstory of the bizarre tragedy of Isaac Babel's uncle Lev, who, "Lassoed by day-dreams, sped along by whips / . . . quit the Pale and lit out for the States / with all the chutzpah of a one-eyed drayman." (29)

Another way *My Hollywood* connects the past to the present is through its use of poetic forms. A pentameterized version of the usual tetrameter Onegin sonnet seems a particular favorite of Dralyuk's (there are ten of them in this relatively brief collection). And there is a certain aptness in his repeated employment of the Onegin sonnet—from Pushkin's great Russian poem of romance and ennui—to depict (as he frequently does) L.A.'s Russian-speaking émigré community. Dralyuk uses a variety of other received forms as well, including a villanelle, a pantoum, a ballade, and various rhymed stanzas. Whatever the form, rhyme pervades these poems. Whether brief or longer (one can't quite say long, since even his few sequences rarely reach beyond fifty lines), there's hardly a poem or translation that doesn't include rhyme in some way. There is also something to be said for the variety and quality of the rhymes, both full and slant. A few that come to mind for their ingenuity and playfulness with language include "lend us / haciendas," (23) "aloes / gallows" (21) and "ante / plenty" (24). These and others attest to the depth of Dralyuk's sonic imagination.

The book's third section, "Russian Hollywood," is devoted entirely to translations of five lesser-known Russophone poets, all of them once exiles in L.A. (Dralyuk, who himself emigrated to the US from Ukraine as a boy, is also a prolific translator of prose fiction from Russian into English.) The placement of these translations alongside Dralyuk's own poems recalls a bygone era when American poet-translators such as Richard Wilbur and W. D. Snodgrass would often include translations in their collections—a practice that, rather bafflingly, has waned in recent years, even while translation itself has flourished among American poets.

Another unfashionable but vital poetic tradition Dralyuk contributes to is the composition of epigrams—a practice that once prospered among mid-century verse masters such as J. V. Cunningham, Howard Nemerov, and John Frederick Nims. The handful of epigrams included in this book are of such a fine quality as to qualify Dralyuk as a contemporary master of the form. One of the best of these, "Old Flame," is a mere quatrain in length:

> Above the tongue-tip is an air so blue
> I can compare it only to how you,
> who once consumed me in a yellow heat,
> now scarcely singe me when we meet.   (39)

Here Dralyuk accomplishes what only the best epigrammatists can, taking an exhausted bit of language—in this case the clichéd moniker for an ex-lover—and reinvigorating it (while also recasting it) through a combination of precise description and metaphor. Such fresh, simultaneous attention to both the literal and the figurative has prompted me to return frequently to "Old Flame" and the other poems in this stunning, durable debut.

Brian Brodeur

On Mistaking a Stranger for a Dead Friend

Bass River, South Yarmouth, Massachusetts

Where dozens of egrets feast
on their own reflection,
late streaks of sun
strike a surfcaster's face.
As he ties a jig lure,
I squint into the glare.

We'd fish this marsh as kids
for perch we called kiver,
a gang of us upriver
stomping swamp orchids
along a tidal island
of storm-washed sand.

In mud boots, I'd hike ahead
to scout a decent spot
on the crook of a silty spit.
Stumbling from a trailhead,
my friend, always last,
would swear he hadn't been lost.

I woke once to his voice,
his boy's voice calling still.
I leaned against the sill,
the window glazed with ice
dripping condensation,
and shut my eyes to listen.

Now, two egrets close
the kinked parentheses
of their necks, a damp breeze
sticking to my clothes.
Low tide's sulfur reek
fouls the estuary.

My friend's father, I learned,
found him in his apartment.
The father, who'd only meant
to stop by on an errand,
folded the typed note
and tried to untie the knot.

Shouldn't *egret* share a root
with *regret*? *Seem* with *seam*?
Swells at tide line gleam,
frothing algae-rot.
Though it urges hush, the surf
will not keep quiet itself.

One stalking egret weaves
through planks of an old pier.
Then, a juvenile pair
wades into grinding waves
that a last piling greets.
The beach crowds with regrets.

— Able Muse Write Prize for Poetry, 2022 ▪ Winner[3]

"'On Mistaking a Stranger for a Dead Friend' has it all—the sounds, the psychology (a whole theory of memory) and, most important of all, playfulness even when the subject is tragic. Bird, riverbank, and a random encounter all blend into a perfect representation of a human mind at work. Bravo!"
  —Aaron Poochigian, Final Judge, 2022 Able Muse Write Prize (for poetry)
    on this winning poem, "On Mistaking a Stranger for a Dead Friend" by Brian Brodeur.

Thomas Mampalam
Measures of Pain and Joy

MAGDALENA HENRIQUEZ GLANCED at the shelves of thick books stacked in the cabinet beside the neurosurgeon's desk. She could distinguish a few of the larger titles. *Brain Tumors, Neurological Critical Care*, and *Vascular Neurosurgery* were three of the prominent texts. Her chronic pain was probably not worth the neurosurgeon's time, she thought. The dark wooden shelves seemed to creak with the weight of the neatly ordered volumes.

She pondered the neurosurgeon's question: "What's your pain on a scale of zero to ten?" Dr. Sid Narayan faced her from his mahogany desk. Behind him, partially opened window blinds framed a filtered view of low green hills and the ash-colored bay. A morning mist hung over the water.

Ten was the torment of a tragic hero, Magdalena thought. The pain was mythological. You were the thief of fire and an eagle tore at your internal organs with beak and talons. Ten was the suffering of the Savior at Golgotha. Only a drama queen would compare their suffering to Prometheus chained to a boulder or Jesus scourged, then nailed to the cross.

Zero was not happiness, but the calm after long meditation in a quiet, dim room. You focused on that stillness and thought of nothing else. One was the tingling from a file of ants crossing your hand on a hot summer day, barely a distraction. You lay on the grass and gazed past the drifting, translucent clouds to the pale blue sky.

Two was a distended stomach after three slices of pizza and a tall soda—more discomfort than pain. With three, a rose thorn pricked your hand as you watered planter boxes in the garden, just a nuisance. Lowering your face to a cluster of flowers, you inhaled.

"Ten would be like a broken bone or maybe like childbirth," Dr. Narayan offered. He noticed wincing at the word *childbirth*.

Just a few seconds passed, but Magdalena knew she should answer soon; she did not want to appear evasive. She also knew that the neurosurgeon had a waiting room full of patients with more serious problems than her neck pain. Brain tumors that caused eyeballs to pop out. Blood vessels about to burst. Bone spurs sticking into spinal cords. Dealing with these misfortunes you clutched the chair arms and worried about how long you had to live or whether you would be paralyzed.

"Ten would be the worst pain you could imagine," Dr. Narayan continued.

She wanted to get the number right. With nine, a pit bull clamped jaws onto your leg, the inquisitor heated a serrated blade to slash across your back, electric shocks coursed down your spine. You thought of nothing but the stabbing pain.

"But you don't have to be screaming or crying for pain to be a ten," he added. "Everyone responds differently."

Four was the tender swelling after a sting from bees that hovered at the yellow and dark red roses in the planter boxes. A doctor would wonder why you were in the office for pain less than four. Eight was the pointed tip of tiger claws or shark jaws. Orange sparks detonated in your mind. For five, a granite boulder you could barely budge balanced on your chest. Your heart beat against the jagged rock. Suffering began here.

She wanted Dr. Narayan to take her pain seriously but not to think she was exaggerating. The number should be above five but modestly under nine.

With seven, you shivered and walked circles in the slush of an icy lake. The pain really focused your attention as you struggled against the bitter chill, barely keeping your head above water. Magdalena hovered beneath this number like those bees at the roses. Her thoughts did a waggle dance. She was close.

"What would six be like?"

Dr. Narayan was not surprised, every clinic morning produced a character. Most patients blurted out the first number that came to mind, but this one made some sort of complex mental calculation. All she had to do was pick a simple whole number. Fractions or irrational numbers were not involved. She spoke perfect English and the intake form indicated she was a teacher at a special needs high school in Oakland, so language was not the problem.

"Maybe this would help." From the desk drawer Dr. Narayan pulled out a chart where line drawings of faces showed increasing levels of pain.

Magdalena saw a series of circles with dots for eyes and curves for smiles or frowns. Zero was a smiley face and ten, a crying face. She then scrutinized Dr. Narayan to make sure he was not mocking her, but saw no sarcasm in his dark brown eyes— even though the chart seemed clearly made for children or brain-damaged adults. His calm tone reassured her.

"Six is the one with the frown but no tears," he said.

"Six seems right," she said. "I feel like a snake squeezes my neck. But I can still breathe and talk."

She thinks best in analogies or metaphors, not numbers or pictures, Dr. Narayan concluded. "There is no right or wrong answer, there is no blood test or device to measure pain. A number is just a simple way to record your pain. You don't have to pick a number."

Magdalena looked confused and again looked closely at the chart. "Six," she said emphatically. "The number is six."

"Good pick," Dr. Narayan said, maybe with some impatience, but, he hoped, not sarcasm.

In the neurological examination Magdalena showed full strength in the major muscle groups and her reflexes were normal as the doctor tapped her elbows and knees with the red rubber tip of the tomahawk shaped hammer. He showed her the MRI scan images of the cervical spine on the desktop computer screen. He counted down the vertebrae and the smooth back edges of the intervening discs. Between the sixth and seventh vertebrae, he saw a small bulge that did not press on the spinal cord or nerves. She was fifty years old; at her age a minor disc bulge was a common degenerative finding.

"The good news is that you don't need surgery," Dr. Narayan said.

So that was it, she thought. He was washing his hands of her just as he washed his hands after removing an old surgical dressing.

"What's the bad news?"

"The bad news is that I don't have a good treatment for your pain."

"Are you saying that the pain is in my head?" She scrunched up her nose as if making another weighty deliberation, maybe this time assigning a number ranking to Dr. Narayan for his error in judgment.

"No. You have pain but you don't need surgery for it."

"Are you saying that I just have to live with this pain for the rest of my life?"

"We have to manage the pain without surgery. I could get one of my colleagues to give you an epidural injection. Would you like to try that?"

There was no surgery in it for him. Magdalena wondered if he was trying to palm her off to another doctor. Consultations were only worthwhile if they led to surgery.

"Sure. I'll try anything if you think it might help."

One month later, Magdalena returned to the office. Again, she sat across from the doctor; behind his head the unchanging gray water of the bay. The injection had not helped. Her pain level was still at a six, a snake squeezing her neck.

Dr. Narayan decided to take another tack. "Is there anything else you want to tell me about your pain?" he asked. "Maybe I missed something."

Magdalena leaned back in her chair, briefly raising her eyebrows. The silence between them seemed long, compelling her to speak.

"Last month was the five-year anniversary of when my son went to heaven."

"Your son died five years ago. How old was he?"

"Twenty-five."

"How did he die?"

"God called him."

Dr. Narayan was not sure if he should push further to make the source of her pain explicit.

"Was it suicide?" Hoping to understand her pain, he wanted to glimpse its source.

She nodded. He said nothing. The how was not important.

She told Dr. Narayan about being at the hair stylist a few blocks from her son's studio. She had missed his call on the cell phone. She heard an ambulance siren but that distant wail was not unusual in their neighborhood.

They sat in more silence and then the doctor said, "I don't have words to help you with that pain. I can only sympathize, I have grown children, too." Magdalena had seen pictures of the neurosurgeon's family in the waiting room. The walls were filled with beautiful framed scenes of marriages, babies, and idyllic vacations to Hawaii and Asia.

"But you think it is all related, that the pain is mostly in my head."

"Grief can manifest as bodily pain. But helping you with that kind of grief is beyond the scope of my practice—you were sent here to see if I recommended surgery on your spine."

"Have you ever experienced pain like I have?" Magdalena knew that even if she walled herself off in a stone tower like a monk, she could never escape it. Only when she was dead and buried would her pain die.

"No. But I do not have to have personal experience with such pain in order to do the right thing by you."

"What is the right thing?" An end to my suffering, she thought.

"You don't need surgery. The pain you suffer for your son needs another kind of attention." He frowned. "Your primary physician could refer you for counseling." It was as if they were in separate rooms. The doctor might have talked longer to Magdalena, but felt he did have to get through the clinic. A craniotomy for resection of a large midline meningioma was scheduled for the afternoon. The residents could start the case but he had to attend for the removal of the tumor off the sagittal venous sinus.

"Your numbers don't describe my pain," Magdalena said. If her son had committed a mortal sin, then the afterlife would bring her no relief.

"I think I understand," said Dr. Narayan. In her world, Magdalena's pain could not be described by a simple integer, but was the product of complex formulae with exponents, radical signs, and limits to infinity. There were asterisks and footnotes with arrows asking for forgiveness, mercy, and deliverance from evil but even with pages of such scrawling, symbols could not contain her pain. Narayan wished that with some magical algebra, he could transform the pain scale into an inverted sequence of joy. Instead of the worst pain imaginable, ten would designate an unattainable bliss, the nirvana of union with God.

"I have not had a moment of happiness since my son died," Magdalena said.

"Maybe if you focus on the good memories, then you can find peace."

"A memory of happiness is not the same as happiness," Magdalena said.

For a moment, Narayan glimpsed discrete joyful images that corresponded to higher integers on the imaginary scale for joy: his wedding to Kamala, the birth of his daughter, Radha, reading to his granddaughter, Maya, in the evenings, the sound of her laughter a silver bell as she splashed in the waves at the seashore or picked strawberries to share from a planter box in the garden. The lower integers were memories of tastes and smells: a dark chocolate, a fruity zinfandel, the fragrance of a dark rose.

"I wish I could have been more helpful to you," Dr. Narayan said.

He walked her to the waiting room. He told his secretary that since Magdalena did not require surgery, she would follow up with her primary care physician.

Turning, Magdalena saw his dark brown eyes and then the soft brown eyes of her son. She envisaged the Savior crowned with thorns and wrapped in a purple robe, his face smeared with tears, sweat, and blood, but made beautiful through endurance. The Savior's sorrowful eyes told her he shared each person's suffering even if silently.

"Thank you for asking if there was anything else," she said.

"I wish the best for your future, "Dr. Narayan said. "I will call your primary care physician about referring you for counseling."

As he walked back to his office he thought that office conversations barely touched the particular quality of each patient's pain. Only a few could be cured and for many the best he could do was avoid worsening their misery. He had to let go and move on to the next case. He really could not measure pain, let alone joy.

Susan McLean

A Review of Alexandra Oliver,
Hail, the Invisible Watchman

Biblioasis; First edition (April 12, 2022)
ISBN 978-1-77196-471-5, 80 pp., USA $15.95, paperback

★ ★ ★

BOTH SATIRICAL POETRY and narrative poetry are currently out of fashion (the former more than the latter), but if you are a formalist, you have shown that you don't care about fashions in poetry, so you may as well go all the way and write what you like. Alexandra Oliver, in *Hail, the Invisible Watchman* (Biblioasis, 2022), shows off her bravura poetic technique and her sharp satiric eye, extending her darkly ironic visions from the individual poems that populated her first two collections, to the more novelistic narrative mosaics in her latest book.

A Canadian poet who started out in slam poetry in the 1990s, Oliver coedited the poetry journal the *Rotary Dial* with Pino Coluccio, and *Measure for Measure: An Anthology of Poetic Meters* (2015) with Annie Finch. Her two previous full-length poetry collections were *Meeting the Tormentors in Safeway* (Biblioasis, 2013), which won the Pat Lowther Award for the year's best poetry book by a Canadian woman, and *Let the Empire Down* (Biblioasis, 2016), which was a finalist for the same award.

Her latest book is organized into three sections. The first, "The Haunting of Sherbet Lake," is the most eclectic; it is reminiscent of Edgar Lee Masters's *Spoon River Anthology* in the way that individual poems' portraits of different members of a community create a vivid picture of the community as a whole. Whereas Masters's individual voices were of those who were already dead, Oliver's are alive but often seem spiritually dead, acting out scenarios of political ambition ("Young Politician at a Rotary Club Tea"), social snobbery ("Song of the Doyenne"), the mutual disdain of a sneering teacher and insolent students ("Schoolteacher Report I [2016]" and "Schoolteacher Report II [1975/2013]"), or the inchoate yearning for something different that attracts daughters to a darkness that will ruin them ("The Vampire Lovers"). This section, though, is not locked into just one theme: for instance, there is an amusing pastiche of Robert Browning called "The Last Straw of the Last Duchess," in which a very contemporary-sounding teenager doesn't understand why her older husband can't just chill and accept her as she is: "I'm just a *people person*, that's my point. / I'm sorry if his nose is out of joint." Other poems include an analysis of why women who feel tired or bored or rattled by change tend to buy a new lipstick ("The Lipstick Effect"), and why it's so easy to make friends when you are young and single, but so hard when you have moved to suburbia, and the only people you meet are like "the flat-eyed school-gate falcon, / studded bright with the nails of a moneyed marriage" ("The Creatures").

The second section, "The Blood of the Jagers," starts with a list of "Dramatis Personae," suggesting that a play is forthcoming. There are five characters—a mother, a father, a son, a daughter, and the son's wife—but only the three women have speaking roles. In poetic monologues, they take turns narrating the family's clashes and disappointments. The scenarios are familiar from family dramas: the mother favors the son and the father favors the daughter, but the father dies early and the son's addictions turn him into a terror for his mother and his foreign-born wife Anu, whom he abuses. The mother, Anaïs, seen mainly through her daughter Ottilie's eyes, is a hard-drinking, brittle socialite, who takes out her frustrations by grabbing the pacifier from a toddler in a passing stroller, saying "*Scream as loud as you want*" ("Lobby"). When her four-year-old daughter turns a hose on the well-coiffed mother, she smacks her to the ground, insisting "The child had it coming" ("Hose"). But when her cocaine-addicted son attacks her in her old age, she brains him with her cane and escapes to the neighbors ("The Barbarian Invasion").

In one of the most lyrical poems of this section ("Best Practice"), Ottilie says:

> We thought it would be over soon enough.
> He'd listen to the facts and move along,
> find a job, a house, someone to love,
> but we were wrong.

The rest of the poem recounts how other "punk lords of misrule" aged into responsible husbands and fathers while her brother Simon

> wouldn't ever soften
> but curled his evils into my life and yours
> and that is why our mother says so often
> *Check the doors.*

114

Ottilie, in "Epilogue: Her Mustang," looking at the fearful, defeated woman her mother has become, wishes that her mother could go back to 1975, "climb into her Mustang" and "drive off, and leave the mess we are behind." But clearly the mess is as much of the mother's making as of any of the others. Ottilie, who is the speaker in the majority of the poems, is the one least defined. She reveals a couple of vignettes from her childhood, but nothing of her adult life. It's a bleak story, but well told, with a ream of novelistic detail and enough left unsaid to let the reader participate in piecing the puzzle together, rather than just watching it unfold.

The third section is the most problematic, because it is a narrative sonnet sequence based on a Canadian novel by Ethel Wilson, *Hetty Dorval* (1947), that may still have readers in Canada, but is not well known elsewhere. Oliver's endnotes contain a brief synopsis of the novel, which is helpful, but does not entirely succeed in turning the sonnet sequence into a coherent story for readers who are not already familiar with it. Most of the sonnets are narrated by a young girl, Frankie, though some are in the voice of an omniscient narrator, and one is in the voice of Mrs. Broom, who appears to be Hetty's housekeeper. Hetty herself is a beautiful young divorcée of mysterious background and questionable reputation who moves to a small community in inland British Columbia and charms Frankie, a local girl. Frankie's parents, alarmed by the woman's undefined status and unusually free behavior, separate their daughter from Hetty. Frankie later rejects Hetty, while still acknowledging her power to charm, and Hetty goes on to marry two men, first a British lord and then a Jewish businessman in Vienna, the latter suggesting future doom for Hetty in the coming World War II.

In her second book of poetry, *Let the Empire Down*, Oliver included a section, "Movies," in which she gave her own poetic takes on well-known art films, especially those by Fellini (*La Dolce Vita, 8 ½, Satyricon, La Strada*), but also Michael Haneke's *The White Ribbon*, Wong Kar-Wei's *In the Mood for Love*, and Luca Guadagnino's *Suspiria*. Poems about literary or artistic works can succeed or fail in a number of ways. If the original work that inspired the poem is not known to the reader, the poet's take on it may sound intriguing enough to make readers want to experience the original. If readers do know the original, they may be able not only to catch the allusions to particular aspects of it, but also to recognize when the poet is presenting a unique take on them. On the other hand, readers who do not know the original work (or do not remember it clearly) may not be able to follow the author's elliptical allusions to it, much less realize when the poet is interpreting rather than describing. In short, such poems are sometimes mysteries to which readers may or may not have the key.

For me, such confusion was the case with Oliver's sonnets about *Hetty Dorval*. The plot synopsis, though helpful in setting out the overall arc of the story, was not much help in the "What happens and when?" elucidation of the plot, so each individual sonnet feels more like a clip from a movie trailer than a narrative. The sonnets are elegantly written, and some of the linking symbols, such as the vee of wild geese as an embodiment of the untamed natural freedom of Hetty, are effective. Oliver makes it clear that she sees Frankie's ultimate rejection of Hetty not as a triumph of experience over naïve admiration, but as a betrayal of Frankie's own truest self in favor of the judgmental conventions of a sexist society.

Is it a mistake to write a series of sonnets about a book that is probably familiar mainly to Canadians, and within that group, more likely to female than to male readers? It depends on the author's goals. All poetry books are targeting niche readers, mainly other poets. There is nothing wrong with Oliver's goal of bringing attention to a novel that she describes as "much-misunderstood (and underrated)" (*Hail* 84). Most readers who do not already know the novel will still be able to follow the general drift of the plot, even if certain details leave them mystified. If Oliver's goal is to entice readers to read the novel, she may be successful in some cases. But readers will vary in the extent to which they are willing to remain suspended in uncertainty versus feeling that they can fully follow the narrative.

All readers are likely to agree that Oliver's command of rhyme and meter are impressive. The many sonnets are in flexible, conversational iambic meter, with deft use of enjambment and punctuation to vary the rhythms. She is equally adept at slant rhyme and true rhyme, and at Petrarchan and Shakespearean rhyme schemes, and she often experiments with rare rhyming patterns. "Pierogis" is written in five ten-line stanzas, each with a rhyme scheme of ABCDEEDCBA. This mirror rhyme scheme is one of Oliver's signature moves. It appears also in the eight-line stanzas of "Triptych: American Wives," in the fourteen lines of "Hose," in the ten-line stanzas of "The Marine Room" and "Family Standards," and in the six-line stanzas of "Neighbourhood Watch." It has long been a favorite approach for her. In *Meeting the Tormentors in Safeway*, she used it in the eight-line stanzas of "The Promise We Made to the Earthquake" and "What You Want the Doctor to Tell You," and the ten-line stanzas of "A Child's Christmas in the Socialist Federal Republic of Yugoslavia." It also appeared in *Let the Empire Down*, in the eight-line stanzas of "Photo Taken Before a Mugging: Florence, July 1976" and "The Vanishing," the ten-line stanzas of "The Prediction," and the fourteen-line stanzas of "Plans."

A mirror rhyme scheme in long stanzas increases the challenge of writing them, because it is harder to plan ahead as the distances between the rhymes grow greater. Yet such a scheme is less immediately pleasurable to readers or listeners because it is harder to hear or notice rhymes that are far apart, especially if they are also slant. In particular, the sense of closure that rhyme can provide is much less likely to add to the power of an ending if one has to look back eight lines or more to notice it. As formalists know, following any regular pattern can be helpful in composing a poem, partly because it forces the poet to try harder and not accept the first wording that comes to mind. The rhymes themselves also can suggest ideas and images that might not otherwise have occurred to the writer.

Although Oliver's long mirror stanzas impress with their sheer technical difficulty, often the hypnotic, songlike effect of shorter, true-rhymed stanzas delights most memorably. In *Meeting the Tormentors in Safeway*, for instance, "The Classics Lesson" starts:

> I told him about Galatea,
> the joyful, animated queen.
> He told me, *make it short—I have*
> *three discs of porn I haven't seen.*

The poem continues through more stanzas in which the speaker recounts the way Pygmalion's love for the female statue he sculpted brings it to life, with the speaker constantly being interrupted by dismissive comments from the male listener, until it ends with him walking out to get more cigarettes from the store:

> He told me, *I forgot my keys.*
> He told me, *hey, it's ten below.*
> He told me, *open this damn door.*
> I told him no. I told him no. (*Meeting* 26–27)

The "lesson" of the title has taken on a witty new meaning by the end of the poem, but I would argue that the force of the reversal is amplified by the emphatic rhymes, making it one of the most memorable poems in that book.

Likewise, in *Let the Empire Down*, one of the standout poems is "Margaret Rose," about Queen Elizabeth II's sister, which starts

> The females of my family extolled
> the virtues of our Queen, her cautious charm,
> the opera glove that sheathed her guiding arm.
> For this was ours, the Englishwoman's mould.

The Queen's discretion and her sister's mistakes are contrasted in the succeeding stanzas, until in the concluding two stanzas,

> The E2 tank slides onward into battle,
> waving stiffly from the Bentley's back,
> warning certain women not to crack,
> waiting for the rabble dust to settle—
>
> while Margaret, taut and disappointed,
> has sunk like squandered change into the shoals,
> but in the murk, her eyes glow, purple coals.
> To us, the normal, she is God's anointed. (*Let* 13)

Although the poem endorses Margaret's relatable failure over the Queen's decorous success, its quatrains roll on like "the E2 tank," unstoppably powerful. When Oliver harnesses the power of full rhyme in tight formation, as she does here, the effect is riveting.

Oliver is adventurous in her formalism. On the one hand, she pairs standard forms with nonstandard content. "Bacon," in *Hail, the Invisible Watchman*, is a villanelle in which a lustful middle-aged man writes to a seventeen-year-old girl in Germany who had posted on Twitter, "I'm wearing a micro-skirt and my bacon is stuck to the chair." On the other hand, she experiments with less commonly used meters, often to contrast the tone of the content with the mood inspired by the rhythm. By writing in lilting anapests, she lightens her savage satire of a rich woman who courts and cows the neighboring women ("Song of the Doyenne"). She tries out the rarely used dactylic meter for "The Vampire Lovers," in which the falling rhythms contribute to the sinister hints of doom in the content. In "Grass" she uses an even odder rhyme scheme than her mirror stanzas, rhyming across stanzas instead of within them: ABCDEF ABCDEF. Such a rhyme scheme is even less likely to be picked up by most readers than her long mirror-rhyme schemes, but they show a mind restlessly trying new things in order to discover new effects. Not everything works, but it is not boring to watch such inventiveness in action. Her biggest formal risk is in the extended sonnet sequence on *Hetty Dorval*, in which putting fourteen Shakespearean sonnets in a row may feel like too much of the same thing to some readers.

What Oliver does best is satire with an edge. Her mordant, cynical attitude is visible in poems about everything from ambitious dads taking their eight-year-old daughters to grueling sports training ("Seventeen") to neighbors who note signs of possible abuse in a family, but choose to be "discreet" about the family's problems ("Neighbourhood Watch"). However, the indignation and censure implied in such poems are tempered by an awareness that these patterns are part of the human condition, and by a sad sense of the loss of happiness that results from them. Part of Oliver is sympathetic to wrecked nihilists who want to destroy the whole rotten system, as in her poem "She Burns the Motel." But another part of her is the one who writes the poems, and writing them is an effort to improve our flawed world, one reader at a time.

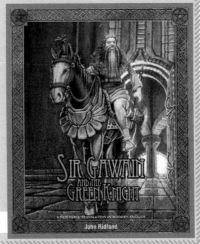

TRANSLATION NOTES

Dobór naturalny

Po latach eliminacji bezwartościowych osobników
Powstał wreszcie gatunek który odżywiał się opakowaniami
Po czipsach, z przyjemnością oglądał reklamy
Maści na hemoroidy i transmisje z zamieszek na Marsie
Uwielbiał spacery z sąsiadem na smyczy
Rozmnażał się wirtualnie przez lajkowanie
Kochał dorodne piksele i poranny smog
Na szczęście Bóg nie miał z tym nic wspólnego

> — *Tadeusz Dziewanowski*
> *(Polish original of "Natural Selection" on page 13)*

Corporeality
~ Stories by Hollis Seamon

978-1-927409-03-9 | Paperback

- **Gold Medal winner, 2014 Independent Book Publisher Outstanding Book Award**
- **Finalist, 2013 Foreword Review's Best Book of the Year**

"Seamon offers enough thematic and narrative variation to keep each story in this collection fresh."— *Publishers Weekly*

Sailing to Babylon
~ Poems by James Pollock

978-0-9865338-7-7 | Paperback

- **Winner, Outstanding Achievement Award in Poetry from the Wisconsin Library Association**
- **Finalist, 2013 Griffin Poetry Prize**
- **Finalist, 2012 Governor General's Literary Award in Poetry**
- **Honorable Mention, 2012 Posner Poetry Book Award**

"A rich and complex array of subjects and allusions to provide both pleasure and challenge."— *Pleiades: A Journal of New Writing*

Strange Borderlands
~ Poems by Ben Berman

978-1-927409-05-3 | Paperback

- **Winner, 2014 Peace Corps Writers Best Book Award**

- **Finalist, 2014 Massachusetts Book Award**

"This is a must-have book for readers of poetry."
— *Publishers Weekly,* starred review

Life in the Second Circle
~ Poems by Michael Cantor

978-0-9878705-5-1 | Paperback

Finalist, 2013 Massachusetts Book Award

"A sensory kaleidoscope where the poems are more like movies."
— Deborah Warren

Bad Fame

~ Poems by Martin McGovern

978-1-927409-50-3 | Paperback

Finalist, 2016 Colorado Book Award

"Martin McGovern's long-awaited, well-constructed first book . . . is carefully considered, quietly passionate, and deeply humane."
—Edward Hirsch

Cup

~ Poems by Jeredith Merrin

SPECIAL HONOREE – 2013 ABLE MUSE BOOK AWARD

978-1-927409-34-3 | Paperback

Finalist, 2015 New Mexico-Arizona Book Award

"In *Cup* we meet a poet of rare power and unique originality."
— X. J. Kennedy

The Cosmic Purr

~ Poems by
Aaron Poochigian

978-0-9878705-2-0 |
Paperback

**Shortlisted,
2014 Poets Prize**

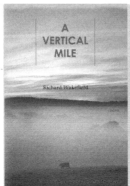

A Vertical Mile

~ Poems by
Richard Wakefield

978-0-9878705-7-5 |
Paperback

**Shortlisted,
2014 Poets Prize**

Lines of Flight

~ Poems by
Catherine Chandler

978-0-9865338-3-9 |
Paperback

**Shortlisted,
2013 Poets Prize**

Nevertheless

~ Poems by
Wendy Videlock

978-0-9865338-4-6 |
Paperback

**Finalist, 2012
Colorado Book Award**

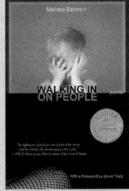
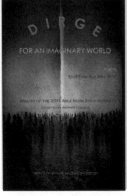

CONTRIBUTOR NOTES

JOHN WALL BARGER's poems and critical writing have appeared in *American Poetry Review, Kenyon Review Online, ZYZZYVA*, the *Cincinnati Review, Poetry Ireland Review*, and *Best of the Best Canadian Poetry*. His sixth book of poems, *Smog Mother*, came out with Palimpsest Press in Fall 2022. He is a contract editor for *Frontenac House*, and teaches in the BFA Program for Creative Writing at the University of the Arts in Philadelphia.

DANIEL BOURNE's books include *The Household Gods, Where No One Spoke the Language*, and the forthcoming *Talking Back to the Exterminator*, from Regal House Publishing. His poems and translations have appeared in *Ploughshares, APR, Field, Boulevard, Guernica, Salmagundi, Yale Review, Pleiades, Shenandoah, Prairie Schooner, Plume, Colorado Review, Virginia Quarterly Review, Quarterly West*, and elsewhere. He has lived in Poland off and on since 1980, including in 1985–87 on a Fulbright fellowship for the translation of underground Polish poets and in 2018 and 2019 for work on an anthology of poets of the Baltic Coast. A collection of his translations of Bronisław Maj, *The Extinction of the Holy City*, is forthcoming from Free Verse Editions in 2023.

BRIAN BRODEUR is the author of four poetry collections, most recently *Some Problems with Autobiography* (Criterion Books, 2023), which won the 2022 New Criterion Prize, and *Every Hour Is Late* (Measure Press, 2019). New poems and literary criticism appear in *Hopkins Review, Gettysburg Review, Los Angeles Review of Books, Southern Review*, and the *Writer's Chronicle*. Brian lives with his wife and daughter in the Whitewater River Valley. He teaches at Indiana University East.

L. M. Brown's short story collections *Treading The Uneven Road* (Fomite 2019) and *Were We Awake* (Fomite 2019) were both featured on *World Literature Today*. She has two novels published. Her latest novel *Hinterland* (Fomite 2020) was an honorable mention finalist in the Eric Hoffer Award (2021). Her short stories have won the Able Muse Write Prize for Fiction in 2020 and 2022, and have been shortlisted for the Bath Short Story Award, SmokeLong Quarterly Flash Fiction Award, Fractured Lit Award, and published in over a dozen literary magazines, such as *Los Angeles Review, Eclectica*, the *Chiron Review, Review Americana, Fiction Southeast, Litro*, and more. She grew up in Ireland but lives in Massachusetts with her husband and three daughters.

BLAKE CAMPBELL's writing has appeared in *Painted Bride Quarterly*, the *Dark Horse*, the *Worcester Review, Measure Review, Lambda Literary*, and the anthology *14 International Younger Poets*. A Pushcart Prize nominee, he is the recipient of the 2015 Aliki Perroti and Seth Frank Most Promising Young Poet Award from the Academy of American Poets and a 2020 Emerging Artist Award from the St. Botolph Club Foundation. "Numinous Rooms," his poem in this issue, was inspired by the painting *The Numinous Room* by the late artist Quinton Oliver Jones, of Salem, Massachusetts. Campbell's chapbook, *Across the Creek*, is available from Pen & Anvil Press.

DAN CAMPION is the author of *Peter De Vries and Surrealism* and coeditor of *Walt Whitman: The Measure of His Song*, a third edition of which was issued in 2019. His poems have appeared previously in *Able Muse* and widely in other publications. A selection of his verse is gathered in *A Playbill for Sunset*, issued by Ice Cube Press in July 2022. He lives in Iowa City, Iowa.

MIKE CHASAR is the author of *Poetry Unbound: Poems and New Media from the Magic Lantern to Instagram* (Columbia UP, 2020) and *Everyday Reading: Poetry and Popular Culture in Modern America* (Columbia UP, 2012), and is coeditor of *Poetry after Cultural Studies* (U of Iowa, 2011). He was a National Endowment for the Humanities Fellow in 2016 and a Kluge Fellow at the Library of Congress in 2015. He teaches at Willamette University in Salem, Oregon.

BROOKE CLARK is the book review editor for *Able Muse* and the author of the poetry collection *Urbanities* (Fitzhenry & Whiteside, 2020). He is also the editor of the epigram website the *Asses of Parnassus*.

TERESE COE'S poems, translations, and prose appear in many international journals including *Able Muse, Agenda, Alaska Quarterly, American Arts Quarterly, Cincinnati Review, Classical Outlook, Crannog, Cyphers, Hopkins Review, Metamorphoses*, the *Moth, New American Writing, New Scotland Writing, Ploughshares, Poetry, Poetry Review, Stinging Fly, Threepenny Review*, and the *TLS*. Her collection *Shot Silk* was shortlisted for the 2017 Poets Prize, and her poem "More" was among those heli-dropped across London for the 2012 Olympics Rain of Poems.

SILVIA DIPIERDOMENICO is an Italian teacher and private tutor. Her previous publications include a work of literary nonfiction in *McSweeney's Quarterly* and an essay in *Elle Magazine*. Raised bilingually in Central Massachusetts, she completed a BA in English at Yale University, where she continued her studies and received an MA and MPhil in Italian literature. While living in New York City, she taught Italian at the Fashion Institute of Technology. Currently settled in Los Angeles, she lives with her husband and their Swiss White Shepherd dog, Fia.

Born in Gdańsk in 1953, TADEUSZ DZIEWANOWSKI was involved in Polish street theater as both a writer and performer during the 1970s, and was a cofounder of the Gdańsk-area creative group, Tawerna Psychonautów (The Tavern of the Psychonauts), in the 1980s. More recently, he has been a poet and translator from English. His first book of poetry, *Siedemnaście tysięcy małpich ogonów* (*Seventeen Thousand Monkey Tales*), appeared in 2009, and his poetry, reviews, and translations from English appear regularly in the Polish literary journal *Topos*. In the US, Daniel Bourne's translations of his poetry have appeared in *Plume* (including in their bilingual collaborative poetry project "A Journey Between the Lands"), *International Poetry Review*, the *Sow's Ear Poetry Review*, and elsewhere.

EVAN FISCELLA is a non-binary person who uses they/them pronouns. They were born in New York and currently live in Boston. They write about their struggles with mental health and addiction.

AARON FISCHER worked for forty years as a print and online editor for newspapers and magazines. His poems have appeared in the *American Journal of Poetry, Briar Cliff Review, Crosswinds Poetry Journal, Five Points, Hudson Review, Naugatuck River Review*, and elsewhere. He won the 2020 Prime Number Magazine Awards for Poetry, as well as the Laureates' Choice from the Maria W. Faust Sonnet Contest for 2019 and 2021. His chapbook, *Black Stars of Blood: The Weegee Poems*, comprises ekphrastic poems based on the work of the great news photographer of the thirties and forties. Fischer was the founding rhythm guitarist of Trayf, the Jewish punk band.

AMY GLYNN is a poet and essayist whose work appears widely in journals and anthologies including *The Best American Poetry*. Measure Press published her first poetry collection, *A Modern Herbal,* in 2013; her second, *Romance Language*, winner of the 2022 Able Muse Book Award, is forthcoming from Able Muse Press in 2023. She has received the Troubadour Prize, the SPUR Award of the Association of Western Writers, *Poetry Northwest*'s Carolyn Kizer Award, and scholarships to the Sewanee and Bread Loaf Writers Conferences among other honors. She is a two-time James Merrill House Fellow and was the inaugural Poet Laureate for the cities of Orinda and Lafayette, California.

MICHAEL HETTICH has published a dozen books of poetry, most recently *The Mica Mine*, which won the 2020 Lena Shull Book Award from the North Carolina Poetry Society and was published in 2021. A "new and selected" volume is forthcoming from Press 53 in 2023. His poems and essays have appeared in such journals as *Orion, Poetry East, Boulevard, Rattle, Ploughshares*, and *Terrain.org*. He lives in Black Mountain, North Carolina.

STEPHEN KAMPA, the poetry editor for *Able Muse*, holds a BA in English literature from Carleton College and an MFA in poetry from Johns Hopkins University. His first book, *Cracks in the Invisible*, won the 2010 Hollis Summers Poetry Prize and the 2011 Gold Medal in Poetry from the Florida Book Awards. His second book, *Bachelor Pad*, appeared from the Waywiser Press. His poems have also been awarded the Theodore Roethke Prize, first place in the River Styx International Poetry Contest, and four Pushcart nominations. His third collection, *Articulate as Rain*, appeared from Waywiser in 2018. He currently teaches at Flagler College.

TIMOTHY KLEISER is a writer and teacher from Louisville, Kentucky. His writing has appeared in *Atlanta Review, National Review, Modern Age, Still,* *Fathom, Front Porch Republic*, and elsewhere. He is an MFA candidate in poetry at the University of St. Thomas.

JENNA LE is the author of *Six Rivers* (NYQ Books, 2011); *A History of the Cetacean American Diaspora* (Indolent Books, 2017), an Elgin Awards second-place winner, voted on by the international membership of the Science Fiction and Fantasy Poetry Association; and *Manatee Lagoon* (Acre Books, 2022). She is a two-time winner of the Poetry by the Sea Sonnet Contest. Her poems appear in *AGNI, Denver Quarterly, Los Angeles Review, Massachusetts Review, Michigan Quarterly Review, Pleiades, Poet Lore, Verse Daily, West Branch*, and elsewhere. She has a BA in mathematics and an MD, and works as a physician and educator in New York City.

THOMAS MAMPALAM is a board certified neurosurgeon who has practiced in Northern California for over thirty years. He writes poetry and short stories informed by his medical practice, immigration, and family experiences. He has published poems in the *Journal of the American Medical Association, Neurology*, the *Healing Muse, Intima Journal of Narrative Medicine, Ailment: Chronicles of Illness Narratives*, the *Avalon Literary Review, California Quarterly*, the *Cortland Review, Metonym, Good Works Review*, and *Iris Literary Journal*. "Measures of Pain and Joy" is his first published short story.

SUSAN MCLEAN, professor emerita of English at Southwest Minnesota State University, has written three books of poetry: *The Best Disguise*, which won the Richard Wilbur Award, *The Whetstone Misses the Knife*, which won the Donald Justice Poetry Prize, and *Daylight Losing Time*, which is forthcoming from Able Muse Press in 2023. She also has translated a collection of Martial's Latin poems, *Selected Epigrams*, and has served as the translation editor at *Better Than Starbucks*. She lives in Iowa City, Iowa.

BURT MYERS works as an art director in upstate New York. He has had work published recently in the *Southern Review, Barrow Street*, the *Hopkins Review*, and elsewhere.

R. S. POWERS's stories and essays have appeared or are forthcoming in *Sou'wester, Juked, JMWW, Entropy, Speculative Nonfiction, Glimmer Train, X-R-A-Y, World Literature Today*, the *Hunger*, and other journals. He teaches at West Chester University in Pennsylvania.

JAY ROGOFF has published seven collections of poetry, most recently *Loving in Truth: New and Selected Poems* (LSU Press, 2020). His other books include *The Long Fault* (2008), *The Art of Gravity* (2011), and *Enamel Eyes* (2016), all from LSU. His poetry and criticism have appeared in many journals, including the *Georgia Review*, the *Kenyon Review, Salmagundi*, and the *Southern Review*, and he recently completed a thirteen-year stint as dance critic for the *Hopkins Review*. He is at work on a long poem and on a book about George Balanchine's ballets. He lives in Saratoga Springs, New York.

MARY JO SALTER—see page 89.

NATALIE STAPLES earned a BA from Kenyon College and an MFA in Poetry from the University of Oregon. Her work has appeared or is forthcoming in *NPR, Literary Matters, BPR, Terrain.org*, and *SWWIM Every Day*. She serves as the poetry editor for the *Northwest Review*.

N. S. Thompson is the nonfiction editor for *Able Muse* and lives near Oxford, UK. A poet, critic, and translator of Italian fiction, with Andy Croft he edited *A Modern Don Juan: Cantos for These Times by*

Divers Hands (Five Leaves). His poetry publications include *Letter to Auden* (Smokestack Books), *Mr Larkin on Photography* (Red Squirrel), and two recent pamphlets, *After War* (New Walk Editions) and *Ghost Hands* (Melos Press). His translations of Italian poetry can be found in *The Faber Book of 20th Century Italian Poems, Eugenio Montale: Poems* (Penguin), and *Centres of Cataclysm: Fifty Years of Modern Poetry in Translation* (Bloodaxe).

PETER VERTACNIK's work has appeared recently in *32 Poems*, the *New Criterion*, the *Hopkins Review, Literary Matters*, and *THINK*, among others. A finalist for the 2021 Donald Justice Poetry Prize and the 2022 New Criterion Poetry Prize, he currently lives in Florida.

DONALD WHEELOCK's poems have appeared or will appear in *THINK, Ekphrasis, Alabama Literary Review, Blue Unicorn*, and many other publications that welcome formal poetry. His first full-length book of poems, *It's Hard Enough to Fly*, has just been released by Kelsay Books. Although a poet since his thirties, Wheelock's intense immersion in the writing of poetry is relatively recent; his lifelong career has been in music, as a composer of chamber, vocal, and orchestral music. He is professor emeritus of music at Smith College. He lives in Whately, Massachusetts.

GAIL WHITE writes from Breaux Bridge, Louisiana. She is a contributing editor of *Light Poetry Magazine* and has recent poems in *Mezzo Cammin, Better than Starbucks* and *Alabama Literary Review*. Her books, *Asperity Street* (Able Muse Press, 2015) and *Catechism* (White Violet Press, 2016), may be found on Amazon. She loves Victorian novels, Cajun food, and cats.

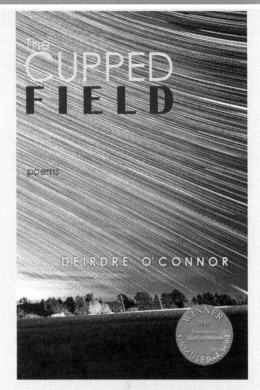

~ *Trap Street*
~ Poems by Will Cordeiro
978-1-77349-057-1 (paperback); 130 pp.

WINNER

2019 Able Muse Book Award

"The formal elegance and beauty of these poems clash smartly with the hardscrabble world where they occur. Back-road towns and landscapes, down-and-out rust belt cities, the worn-out West—this is a book that bears witness to the fizzled American dream." — Maurice Manning, author of Railsplitter

"Trap Street is a map of vanishing dreams, true to the country as it struggles to exist. Yet the person who inhabits these poems has dignified the writing of them with real care and an ear for the elevated vernacular."— David Mason, 2019 Able Muse Book Award judge, author of The Sound

"[T]here is every reason to regard Cordeiro's poems as bridging the gap between life's overlooked detritus and exalted vision itself. And visual acuity here is matched by a strenuous verbality, color-coordinated vowels informing chewable consonants in a lexicon ranging from "cattywampus" to "glumes" to "blear." — Alfred Corn, author of The Poem's Heartbeat

~ *The Cupped Field*
~ Poems by Deirdre O'Connor
978-1-77349-035-9 (paperback); 92 pp.

WINNER

2018 Able Muse Book Award

"Written with great compassion, precision, and nuance, these gorgeously made poems face into the heartbreaks of time and loss, of selves and ex-selves."— Mary Szybist, author of Incarnadine

"Here is a poet who knows that the mind is complex, a map of many countries, in some of which people are starving."— Marilyn Nelson, 2018 Able Muse Book Award judge, author of Faster Than Light

"I am in awe of this poet for many reasons but especially the way she charts a direct line between the mind that takes in the world, in all its beauty and tragedy, and the ethical voice that speaks out of that witness." — Shara McCallum, author of Madwoman

"These are not just good poems. They are spells. . . . Deirdre O'Connor is an exquisite lyric poet." — Ilya Kaminsky, author of Deaf Republic

INDEX

Made in the USA
Columbia, SC
06 January 2023

75735212R00087